Contents

Tables

Figures

1. Summary

Recorded Crime	1.1 The 68,808 notifiable offences recorded by the police in 1995 represented a 1.4% increase compared to 1994 and a 3.8% increase on 1986. Theft is the single largest offence group accounting for 49% of all recorded crime in 1995 compared to 46% in 1986 and 50% in 1991. A total of approximately £44 million of cash and property was stolen in 1995 by way of theft, burglary, robbery, and fraud & forgery, a 21% decrease on the previous year and a 6% decrease on the 1991 figure.

Crime Trends	1.2 In 1995 recorded crime increased in five categories compared to the previous year; sexual offences (up 26%); criminal damage (up 23%); violence against the person (up 7%); other notifiable offences (up 5%) and theft (up 1%). Comparing 1995 with 1986 for the same five offence categories, four have increased; other notifiable offences (up 262%); sexual offences (up 101%); violence against the person (up 64%) and theft (up 9%) and one decreased; criminal damage (down 7%). The increase in other notifiable offences can largely be attributed to recorded drug offences which formed 94% of this category in 1995 compared to 68% in 1991. Four categories of crime decreased between 1994 and 1995; offences against the state (down 23%); fraud and forgery (down 4%); burglary (down 3%) and robbery (down 2%). Compared with 1986, three of these categories also decreased (offences against the state down by 46%; robbery down by 30% and burglary down by 18%) whilst fraud and forgery increased by 16%.

Crime Clear-up	1.3 In 1995 there were 24,838 notifiable offences cleared by the police. This is a 2% increase compared to the number cleared in 1994 and represents an overall clear-up rate of 36% in 1995. The clear-up rate has remained the same in each of the last 3 years. Comparing 1995 with 1986 the number of crimes cleared also rose by 2% whilst the clear-up rate in 1986 at 37% was similar to that of 1995 (36%).

1.4 The offence categories with the highest clear-up rate in 1995 were other notifiable offences, offences against the state and sexual offences (93%; 90%; and 82% respectively). Nearly two thirds of recorded offences of violence against the person and fraud and forgery were cleared. Approximately one third of criminal damage and theft offences were cleared up. The least successful offence categories in terms of crime cleared were burglary and robbery, both with clear-up rates of 19%.

Court Proceedings	1.5 Prosecutions at Magistrates' Courts in 1995 decreased by 3% on 1994. Motoring offences accounted for 59% of all Magistrates' Courts' prosecutions, 2 percentage points below 1994's figure. Indictable and summary offences accounted for 27% and 14% respectively of all Magistrates' Courts' prosecutions compared to 25% and 14% in 1994. The majority of defendants (87%) in 1995 were adult males, 10% were adult females and 3% were juveniles. The number of juvenile defendants in 1995 increased for the third consecutive year. The 1995 figure (1,148) is 35% lower than the 1986 figure (1,759).

1.6 In 1995, the number of Crown Court prosecutions was 1,249, a 3% increase on 1994 but 33% less than 1986. In 1995 91% were adult males. The 1995 total includes 420 persons proceeded against for scheduled offences, which was a 5% increase on 1994, but a 30% decrease on scheduled prosecutions in 1986.

Court Outcomes

1.7 In 1995 88% of defendants at the Magistrates' Court and 86% of defendants at the Crown Court pleaded guilty. Of those pleading not guilty, 88% in Magistrates' Courts and 53% in Crown Courts were acquitted. In 1995, 58% of those convicted in all courts had at least one previous conviction. In terms of gender the highest rate of conviction in 1995 was for males aged 19 years and females aged 19 years.

Sentencing

1.8 In the Crown Court, the most frequently used disposal is immediate custody. This was given to 615 offenders in 1995 - 53% of those found guilty. A further 28% received a suspended custodial sentence, and 10% were given supervision in the community. Conditional discharges accounted for 6% and fines 2% of all Crown Court disposals. Immediate custody continues to be much more prevalent for scheduled offences. In 1995, 66% of scheduled offenders received immediate custody.

1.9 In Magistrates' Courts, a fine is the most common disposal, being given in 1995 to 71% of all offenders (29% of those convicted of indictable offences, 49% of those convicted of summary offences, and 92% of those convicted of motoring offences). During 1995 the proportionate use of the fine was 3 percentage points less than in 1994 (71% compared to 74%). Immediate custodial sentences are much less frequently used than in the Crown Court, reflecting the less serious nature of the offences dealt with. Between 1993 and 1995 the proportionate use of immediate custody in Magistrates' Courts remained unchanged at 5% of all disposals.

1.10 The number of juveniles sentenced by both the Crown Court and Magistrates' Courts in 1995 for indictable and summary offences rose for the third consecutive year. The 1995 figure shows an increase of 16% on 1994 but is 36% less than the number sentenced in 1986. Supervision in the community (36%); a conditional discharge (28%) and immediate custody (23%) are the most frequent disposals given to juveniles in 1995.

The Prison Population

1.11 In 1995 the average daily prison population in Northern Ireland prisons was 1,762, a 7% decrease on the previous year's level of 1,899. Since 1986, the average daily population has fallen by 9%.

1.12 The decrease in the average prison population between 1994 and 1995 is attributable to a fall in both the male population (down 131) and the female population (down 6). The main decrease has been in the average number of remand prisoners (down 122) with smaller decreases in the average number of immediate custody (down 18) and fine default (down 1) prisoners. Interestingly, non-criminal prisoners increased from an average of 1 in 1994 to 5 in 1995.

1.13 Prison receptions increased by 4% between 1994 and 1995. There were increases in both fine default (up 9%) and immediate custody (up 5%) receptions and a 2% decrease in remand prisoner receptions. Overall in 1995, 39% of receptions were of remand prisoners, 31% for fine default, 28% were sentenced to immediate custody and 1% were non-criminal prisoners. The number of non-criminal prisoners received was the highest since 1989.

1.14 In 1995 56% of the average prison population sentenced to immediate custody had committed offences of violence against the person, 13% offences of dishonesty (theft, fraud & forgery, burglary), 11% offences of robbery, 7% sexual offences, 3% drug offences, and 2% criminal damage offences.

2. Notifiable offences recorded by the Police

Introduction

2.1 The recording process for crime normally starts when someone reports to the police that an offence has been committed, when the police discover an offence, or when an offender asks for further offences to be taken into consideration. The police make an initial examination of the facts to determine if there is prima facie evidence that an offence has been committed, and if so a crime report may be filed. If this is the case, and the offence is a serious one, and is contained in a list of notifiable offences prepared by the Home Office, the offence may be recorded for statistical purposes. Less serious offences such as motoring offences, liquor law offences and cruelty to animals are noted by the police and processed without being recorded for statistical purposes.

Counting Rules

2.2 In recording offences the RUC broadly follow Home Office counting rules, issued to ensure as much comparability as possible of figures from different areas and over time. Inevitably some variation does occur. The statistics on notifiable offences incorporate <u>each offence as initially recorded,</u> which may differ from the one for which a suspect or suspects are finally proceeded against. Some offences consist of continuous or repetitive activity; in other cases several people may be the victim of the same criminal act; while some criminal acts may involve the infringement of a number of distinct parts of the criminal law. The Home Office rules specify that, except in special circumstances, only the most serious offence is counted where several offences are committed in one incident. The most serious offence is that which would incur the greatest penalty. Where there was a finding of guilt, the principal offence is usually that for which the greatest penalty was imposed. An exception is made for offences of violence against the person and sexual offences where there is more than one victim, when one offence is usually counted for each victim. Another important concept of the rules is that in the case of a continuous series of offences where there is some special relationship, knowledge or position existing between the offender and the person or property offended against which enables the offender to repeat the offences, only one offence is counted for each continuous offence.

Coverage

2.3 The coverage and categorisation of 'notifiable offences recorded' in this commentary is similar to that of 'notifiable offences' recorded by police forces in England and Wales. An outline of the offences included in each main category, together with an indication of how these differ from those used in England and Wales, is given in Appendix 1. A specific difference from Home Office practice is that criminal damage offences involving under £200 are not recorded in Northern Ireland. All cases, irrespective of the amount involved, are in theory recordable in England and Wales, though this is not always done for cases involving less than £20.

2.4 From 1988 'communication of false information causing a bomb hoax' and 'assault on a constable' are no longer included as notifiable offences, in line with Home Office practice. Data for earlier years have been revised accordingly.

2.5 Offences recorded by public bodies such as the Post Office Investigation Branch, and DHSS are not included, unless they have also been reported to the RUC, or have come to their notice as a result of court proceedings where the defendant may have asked for the offence to be taken into consideration. Prosecutions undertaken by the Department of the Environment in respect of motor tax offences and by the Television Licensing Authority in respect of licence offences are also excluded.

2.6 Statistics of crime recorded by the RUC provide a measure of the amount of crime with which they are faced, but only a partial picture of crime committed. Evidence on the extent of under-reporting is available from victim surveys such as the British Crime Survey (Great Britain), General Household Survey (Great Britain), the Continuous Household Survey (Northern Ireland), the 1992 International Victimisation Survey and the Northern Ireland Crime Survey. These generally indicate that the propensity to report crime is influenced by a number of factors such as offence severity, whether a suspect is known to the victim, the ease with which a report can be made, insurance claim requirements, public attitudes to the police, public attitudes to certain offences (e.g. sexual offences), changes in legislation etc. The British Crime Survey suggests that "incomplete reporting and recording mean that only just over a quarter ...[of comparable crimes]... are estimated to end up in police records"[1]. In general under-reporting is most prevalent for less serious crime with the most serious crimes, such as murder, generally being known to the police. Because the influence of the several factors may vary over time, trends in the number of recorded crimes may differ from trends in the number of crimes committed. Changes in recorded crime, and particularly small year-on-year changes, need to be interpreted with caution.

2.7 At 68,808, the number of recorded offences in 1995 increased on the 1994 level by 1.4% (Table 2.1).

Figure 2.1: NOTIFIABLE OFFENCES RECORDED BY THE POLICE 1986-1995

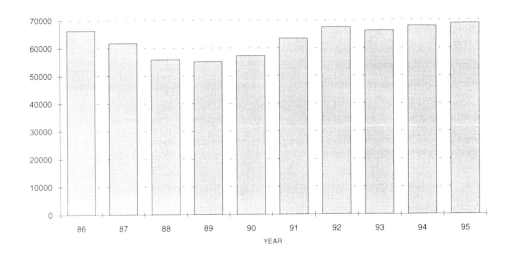

[1] Source: 'Trends in Crime: Findings from the 1994 British Crime Survey'
(Pat Mayhew, Catriona Mirrlees-Black and Natalie Aye Maung),
Research Findings No.14, Home Office Research and Statistics Department, 1994.

2.8 The number of reported crimes in most crime categories increased in 1995 on the previous year. There were increases in sexual offences (up 26%), criminal damage (up 23%), violence against the person (up 7%), other notifiable offences (up 5%) and offences of theft rose slightly (up 1%). By contrast, offences against the state fell (down 23%) as did fraud and forgery (down 4%), burglary (down 3%) and robbery (down 2%). In 1995 as in previous years, theft (49%) and burglary (24%) accounted for approximately three-quarters of all recorded offences.

Figure 2.2: NOTIFIABLE OFFENCES RECORDED 1995

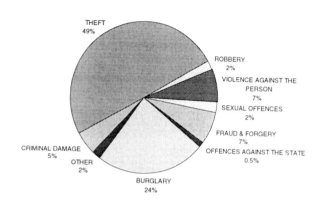

Violent Offences

2.9 Offences of violence against the person recorded by the police in 1995 increased on the previous year to 5,150 (an increase of 7% since 1994). Figure 2.3 shows that murders in 1995 decreased to 22 from 82 in 1994; attempted murders also fell from 255 to 35.

Figure 2.3: NOTIFIABLE OFFENCES OF MURDER AND ATTEMPTED MURDER 1986-1995

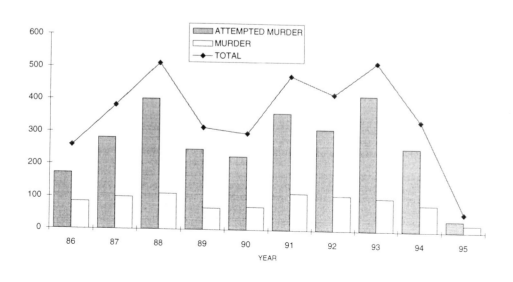

2.10 Sexual offences recorded in 1995 rose to 1,679, an increase of 26% over the previous year. Within the category of sexual offences the number of indecent assaults continued to increase with 932 offences recorded during 1995, 34% up on the figure for the previous year. There was an increase in the number of rapes recorded in 1995 (229) compared to 1994 (168) - an increase of 36%. This increase, combined with a fall of 10 in the number of attempted rapes gives an overall rise in rape related crime of 25% from 1994 to 1995. Incest fell from 24 offences in 1994 to 13 in 1995 and other sexual offences rose 18%.

Figure 2.4: NOTIFIABLE SEXUAL OFFENCES 1986-1995

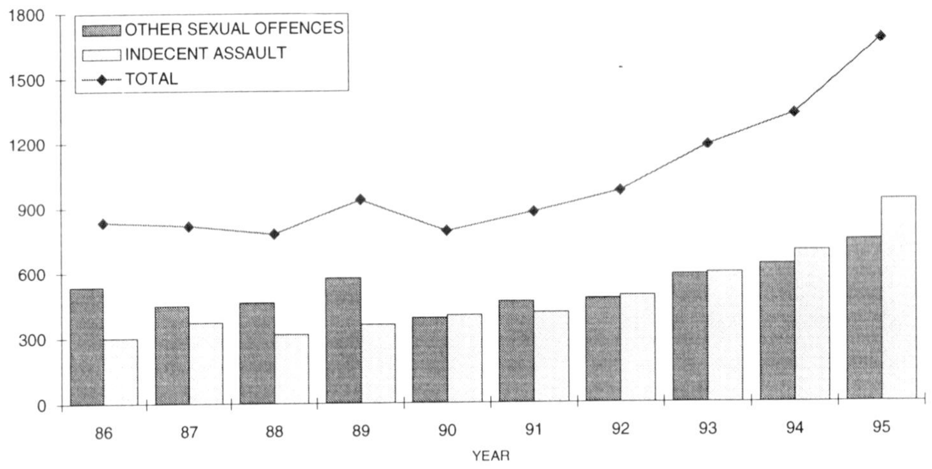

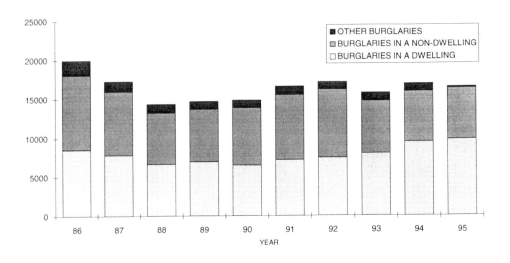

Burglary

2.11 Burglary offences recorded in 1995 dropped to 16,457, a 3% decrease from the 1994 level of 16,902. (See Figure 2.5) More burglaries in 1995 occurred in dwellings (9,774) than in non-dwellings (6,499). It should be noted that from 1995, attempted burglary (previously included in 'other burglary') is now included in burglary in a dwelling or burglary in a non-dwelling. All burglaries accounted for £10.8 million of stolen property and cash.

Figure 2.5: NOTIFIABLE OFFENCES OF BURGLARY 1986-1995

2.12 There were 1,539 robberies recorded in 1995, representing a decrease of 2% from the 1,567 recorded in 1994. This is the lowest figure in the 1986 - 1995 period. The number of hijackings rose by 71% from 194 in 1994 to 331 whilst recorded armed robbery fell by 6% from 657 in 1994 to 620 in 1995. All robberies accounted for £3.2 million of stolen property and cash in 1995.

Figure 2.6: NOTIFIABLE OFFENCES OF ROBBERY 1986-1995

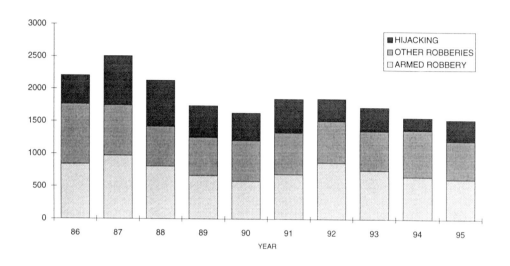

2.13 There were 33,472 thefts recorded in 1995, an increase of 1% (239 crimes) on the 1994 level. A substantial increase of 20% (900) in offences of shoplifting was recorded between 1994 and 1995. Increases were also recorded in theft from dwellings (up 45% to 618 in 1995) and, in theft from the person (up 28% to 330 in 1995). These increases were offset by a large numeric fall in 'car crime' - thefts of and from motor vehicles - a decrease of 1,180 from 1994 to 1995. Shoplifting accounted for 16% of all thefts, a level similar across the 10-year period. £28 million of property and cash was taken by theft in 1995, a decrease of almost 22% (about £7.8 million) over the previous year.

Figure 2.7: NOTIFIABLE OFFENCES OF THEFT 1986-1995

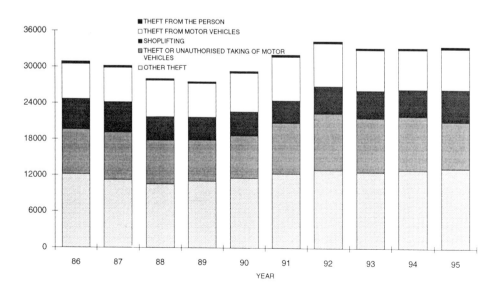

2.14 Offences of fraud and forgery recorded by the police fell in 1995 to 4,884, a fall of 4% on 1994. Over the year the number of forgery offences fell by 30% to stand at 680. This was offset by a 2% increase in the number of frauds recorded in 1995. The financial cost of these offences in 1995 was £1.8 million.

Figure 2.8: NOTIFIABLE OFFENCES OF FRAUD & FORGERY 1986-1995

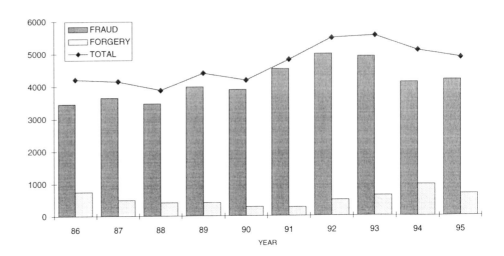

2.15 There were 3,772 offences of criminal damage recorded in 1995. This is a 23% increase on the 1994 level and represents a sixth consecutive annual increase. Arson accounts for approximately one third of such offences, also increasing numerically for the sixth year.

2.16 There were 339 offences against the state recorded in 1995, a 23% decrease on the 1994 figure of 440. This offence category is not the sole quantification of terrorist-type offences which may also be found under other headings (e.g. violence against the person and robbery).

2.17 In the category of 'other notifiable offences' (including kidnapping, drug offences and false imprisonment) in 1995, 1,516 offences were recorded by the police, a 5% increase on the previous year. This increase was largely due to a rise in the number of recorded drug offences from 1,286 in 1994 to 1,426 in 1995; an increase of 11%.

2.18 Police records show that £43.9 million worth of property and cash was stolen in 1995, representing a decrease of £11.7 million from the 1994 level.

Figure 2.9: PROPERTY/CASH STOLEN 1995

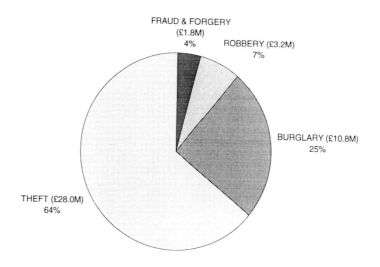

2.19 Table 2.2 shows crime rates per 100,000 population in Northern Ireland and England and Wales over the decade 1986-1995, based on offences defined as 'crime index' offences in the United States of America. This index excludes fraud, criminal damage and offences against the state which are normally included in data for Northern Ireland. On this basis the aggregate crime rate in Northern Ireland for the seven offence categories included in the crime index is less than in England and Wales. Compared to England and Wales, Northern Ireland has a higher rate of rape (including attempted rape) and the same rate of homicide but lower rates in all other categories.

TABLE 2.1: Notifiable offences recorded by the police 1986-1995

CRIME CATEGORY	1986	1987	1988	1989	1990	1991	1992	1993	1994	1995
VIOLENCE AGAINST THE PERSON	3147	3178	3469	3338	3374	3955	4102	4597	4793	5150
Murder	85	100	111	67	71	114	108	101	82	22
Manslaughter & infanticide	2	9	5	8	11	7	3	5	4	2
Attempted murder	173	282	402	247	225	360	311	416	255	35
Other violence against the person	2887	2787	2951	3016	3067	3474	3680	4075	4452	5091
SEXUAL OFFENCES	834	817	779	935	790	877	973	1187	1333	1679
Rape	107	80	94	109	94	117	116	151	168	229
Attempted rape	23	20	20	43	31	38	38	42	40	30
Incest	60	32	34	24	38	25	35	20	24	13
Indecent assault	300	370	317	359	401	413	493	597	698	932
Other sexual offences	344	315	314	400	226	284	291	377	403	475
BURGLARY	19973	17294	14353	14680	14817	16563	17117	15735	16902	16457
Burglary in a dwelling	8545	7844	6655	6967	6505	7206	7461	8005	9454	9774
Burglary in a building other than a dwelling	9532	8098	6583	6691	7311	8281	8677	6675	6480	6499
Other burglary[1]	1896	1352	1115	1022	1001	1076	979	1055	968	184
ROBBERY	2204	2504	2130	1738	1630	1848	1851	1723	1567	1539
Armed robbery	839	969	805	663	579	686	866	751	657	620
Hijacking	444	761	713	487	425	519	339	365	194	331
Other robbery	921	774	612	588	626	643	646	607	716	588
THEFT	30819	30136	27994	27057	29267	32033	34256	33161	33233	33472
Theft from the person	340	284	219	220	219	304	242	217	257	330
Theft in a dwelling	723	634	587	472	428	304	356	436	427	618
Theft from motor vehicles	5784	5679	6058	5626	6443	7227	7117	6729	6555	6715
Shoplifting	5081	5077	3920	3780	3984	3737	4549	4625	4510	5410
Theft or unauthorised taking of motor vehicles	7441	7873	7272	6386	7042	8455	9376	9011	8974	7794
Other thefts	11450	10589	9938	10573	11151	12006	12616	12143	12510	12605
FRAUD & FORGERY	4209	4150	3881	4395	4177	4811	5486	5553	5100	4884
Frauds	3460	3657	3471	3983	3895	4533	4991	4922	4127	4204
Forgery	749	493	410	412	282	278	495	631	973	680
CRIMINAL DAMAGE	4055	2592	2254	2013	2191	2394	2502	2856	3077	3772
Arson	1371	871	773	682	691	805	860	901	940	1132
Explosives offences	79	74	97	81	90	112	117	88	65	13
Other criminal damage [2]	2605	1647	1384	1250	1410	1477	1525	1867	2072	2627
OFFENCES AGAINST THE STATE	624	719	644	626	585	592	478	436	440	339
Offences under the NI Emergency Provisions Act	89	86	124	150	133	151	103	87	106	18
Firearms offences	167	203	178	175	119	114	73	76	98	42
Other offences against the state	368	430	342	301	333	327	302	273	236	279
OTHER NOTIFIABLE OFFENCES	419	389	386	365	367	419	767	980	1441	1516
Drug offences [3]	*	*	*	*	*	287	619	811	1286	1426
Other notifiable offences	419	389	386	365	367	132	148	169	155	90
GRAND TOTAL	66284	61779	55890	55147	57198	63492	67532	66228	67886	68808

Notes:
(1) From 1995 excludes 'Attempted burglary' which is included in 'Burglary in a dwelling' or 'Burglary in a building other than a dwelling'.
(2) Other criminal damage excludes offences where damage was under £200.
(3) Drug offences not available separately prior to 1991 - included in Other notifiable offences.

TABLE 2.2: Crime index offence categories 1986-1995: rate per 100,000 population

	Year	Homicide[1]	Rape [2]	Robbery [3]	Aggravated Assault	Burglary	Larceny Theft	Motor Vehicle Theft[4]
Northern Ireland	1986	6	8	112	195	1275	1492	475
	1987	7	6	111	195	1098	1413	500
	1988	7	7	90	212	910	1313	461
	1989	5	10	79	206	927	1306	403
	1990	5	8	76	207	932	1398	443
	1991	8	10	83	239	1034	1472	528
	1992	7	10	93	247	1058	1537	579
	1993	6	12	83	275	964	1480	552
	1994	5	13	84	287	1030	1478	547
	1995	1	16	73	311	998	1557	473
England & Wales	1986	1	5	60	249	1857	3175	819
	1987	1	5	65	279	1789	3304	774
	1988	1	6	62	312	1620	3099	726
	1989	1	7	65	348	1630	3195	776
	1990	1	7	71	362	1979	3696	972
	1991	1	8	89	371	2386	4265	1139
	1992	1	8	103	392	2643	4419	1142
	1993	1	9	112	397	2663	4198	1152
	1994	1	10	116	423	2437	3930	1024
	1995	1	10	132	418	2401	3776	971

Note: (1)   Includes Murder, Manslaughter and Infanticide - excludes attempts.
(2)   Includes Attempted Rape.
(3)   Excludes Hijacking.
(4)   Excludes Theft from vehicles.

3. Offences cleared by the Police

Introduction

3.1 Broadly an offence, having been recorded for statistical purposes, is said to be cleared if a person has been charged, summonsed, or cautioned for the offence; if the offence is 'taken into consideration' by the court; if there is sufficient evidence to charge a person but the case is not proceeded with because, for example, the suspected offender is under the age of criminal responsibility; or if the suspected offender has died. Because the 'clear-up rate' is conventionally taken as the ratio of offences cleared in a year to the offences recorded in the year and some offences cleared will have been recorded in previous years, clear-up rates may occasionally exceed 100%. They vary considerably for different offences and changes in the overall rate for a major offence category may be due to changes in the proportion of sub-categories within that group. Clear-up rates may also vary because of the nature of the offence. Some offences of violence against the person and some sexual offences have high clear-up rates because the victim can more often readily identify the offender. In the case of some fraud offences the discovery of the offence may identify the offender.

Overall Clear-up

3.2 There were 24,838 notifiable offences cleared by the police in 1995. This represents an increase of 2% (+496) on the 24,342 crimes cleared in 1994. The clear-up rate at 36% remains unchanged from that of 1994. Clear-up rates had been steadily improving up to a record high of 45% in 1988 (25,226) after which they fell and have remained constant at 36% since 1993.

Figure 3.1: CRIMES RECORDED AS CLEARED 1986-1995

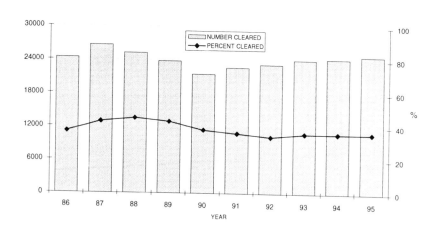

3.3 Trends in clear-up rates for individual categories of crime can be seen in Table 3.1.

Offence types

3.4 Offence groups which typically demonstrate high clear-up rates are other offences, sexual offences, offences against the state, violence against the person and offences involving fraud or forgery. Rates for 1995 are 93%, 82%, 90%, 67% and 63% respectively.

Figure 3.2: CRIMES CLEARED: SEXUAL OFFENCES 1986-1995

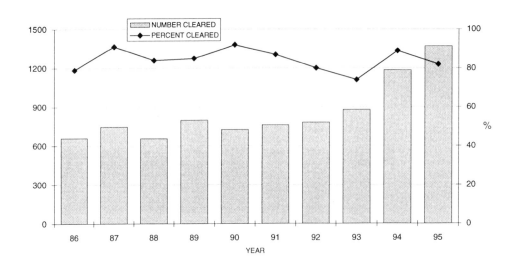

Figure 3.3: CRIMES CLEARED: OFFENCES AGAINST THE STATE 1986-1995

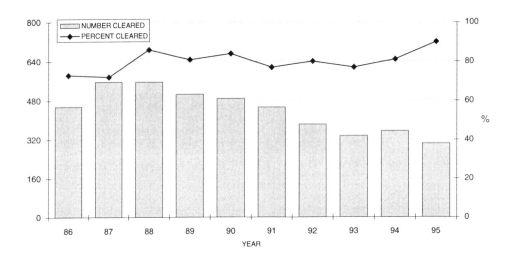

Figure 3.4: CRIMES CLEARED: VIOLENCE AGAINST THE PERSON 1986-1995

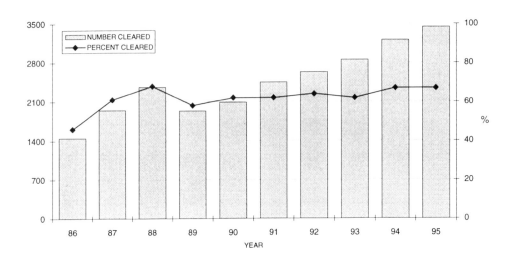

Figure 3.5: CRIMES CLEARED: FRAUD AND FORGERY 1986-1995

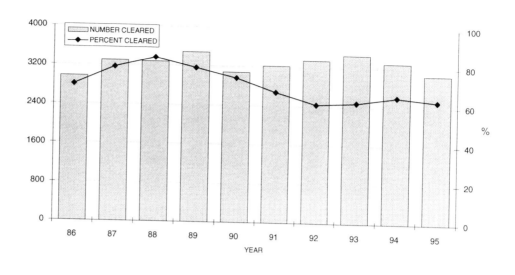

3.5 Offences which are currently and historically less successfully cleared up are recorded offences of theft and criminal damage. Approximately one third of such offences were cleared up in 1995. The respective 1994 and 1995 clear-up rates for theft (31%) are the lowest rates in the last decade. The clear-up rate for criminal damage improved in 1993 (35%) and 1994 (36%) but fell to 33% in 1995. The 1995 clear-up rate for criminal damage is 2 percentage points higher than that for 1986 (31%).

Figure 3.6: CRIMES CLEARED: THEFT 1986-1995

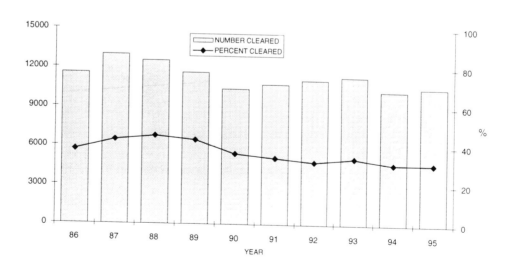

Figure 3.7: CRIMES CLEARED: CRIMINAL DAMAGE 1986-1995

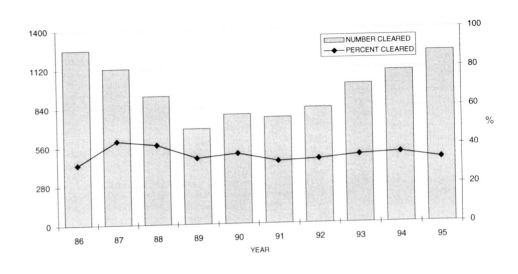

3.6 Offences which have the lowest clear-up rates both currently and historically are burglary and robbery, with 19% of both categories respectively being cleared in 1995. The clear-up rate for burglary (19%) in 1995 equals the lowest rate in the 1986-1995 period (19% in 1992) but is seven percentage points less than in 1986 (26%). The clear-up rate for robbery in 1995 (19%) is the same as in 1986. Robbery clear-up rates have ranged from a low of 15% in 1993 to a high of 23% in 1988 during the 1986-1995 period.

Figure 3.8: CRIMES CLEARED: BURGLARY 1986-1995

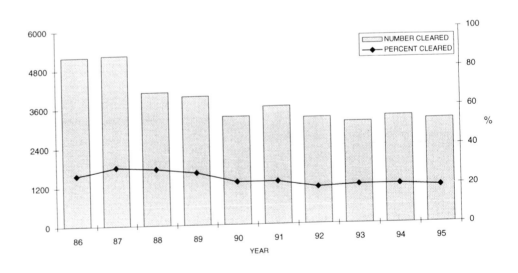

Figure 3.9: CRIMES CLEARED: ROBBERY 1986-1995

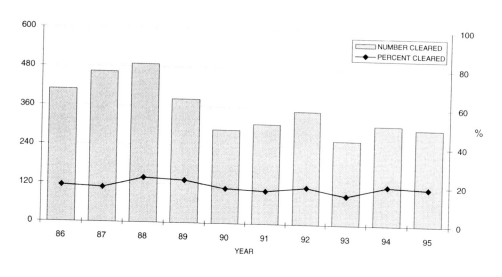

3.7 The Northern Ireland clear-up rate increased from 37% in 1986 to 45% in 1988, it then fell to 34% in 1992 but rose again to 36% in 1993 and has remained the same for 1994 and 1995. This compares favourably to the levels for England and Wales which have been on average 10 percentage points below Northern Ireland for the same period. The clear-up rate rose from 32% in 1986 to 35% in 1988 but fell back to 25% in 1993 and has remained at 26% for both 1994 and 1995.

3.8 A comparison of changes in the actual number of crimes cleared between Northern Ireland and England and Wales is interesting. From 1994 to 1995 there was a 2% increase in the numbers of crime cleared in Northern Ireland but a 4% decrease in England and Wales. The fall in the number of crimes cleared up in England and Wales however was offset by a decrease in the number of crimes reported to the police (down 2%). The clear-up rate remained at 26%. In Northern Ireland the 1995 clear-up rate of 36% compares well with police forces in England and Wales. Only 4 police forces out of 43 had higher clear-up rates than the Royal Ulster Constabulary. Two of these police forces were in Wales.

3.9 A comparison of method of clear-up between Northern Ireland and England and Wales over the 1985-95 period illustrates differences in clear-up patterns. In England and Wales the proportion of crimes cleared up through individuals being charged rose gradually from 50% in 1985 to 53% in 1989 before three successive decreases to 46% in 1992. It stayed at this rate in 1993, dropped to 45% in 1994 and then further again to 44% in 1995. The rate for Northern Ireland is typically higher although again has shown a reduction in recent years falling from 62% in 1985 to 50% in 1995.

3.10 In both jurisdictions the proportionate rates of clear-up by the use of cautioning also provide interesting comparisons. In England and Wales the proportion has decreased from 13% in 1985 to 10% in 1986 rising to 15% in 1993. It decreased slightly to 14% in 1994 and remained the same in 1995. In Northern Ireland the rate gradually increased from 8% to 16% during the same period. However, it should be noted that in Northern Ireland offences cleared by 'caution' may include some cases where advice and warnings are given to juveniles. This is not the case in England and Wales.

3.11 Looking for consistent trends between the two areas in relation to offences taken into consideration (TIC) as method of clear-up is not as straightforward. Over the 1985-89 period the proportion in Northern Ireland fluctuated slightly but remained relatively constant at about 15% before dropping to 10% in 1990. This proportion remained relatively constant until a decrease to 5% in 1994 and then to 4% in 1995. The proportion for England and Wales has declined from 1985 to 1992 but with no real discernible pattern. 1985-87 saw a decrease from 19% to 16%, followed by a rise (to 17%) in 1988. This was followed by a drop (to 13%) in 1989, followed by two consecutive rises to 18% in 1991 before 4 consecutive decreases to 10% in 1995. It would appear that in 1995, the RUC made proportionately greater use of charges, approximately the same use of the caution, and had fewer offences cleared-up by the TIC procedure than their counterparts in England and Wales.

TABLE 3.1: Crimes recorded and crimes cleared by the police 1986-1995

CRIME CATEGORY	1986	1987	1988	1989	1990	1991	1992	1993	1994	1995
Notifiable crimes recorded	66284	61779	55890	55147	57198	63492	67532	66228	67886	68808
Number of crimes cleared	24344	26617	25226	23808	21475	22675	23253	24088	24342	24838
Clear-up rate (%)	37	43	45	43	38	36	34	36	36	36

TABLE 3.2: Notifiable offences cleared by the police as a percentage of those recorded 1986-1995

CRIME CATEGORY	1986 (%)	1987 (%)	1988 (%)	1989 (%)	1990 (%)	1991 (%)	1992 (%)	1993 (%)	1994 (%)	1995 (%)
VIOLENCE AGAINST THE PERSON	46	61	68	58	62	62	64	62	67	67
Murder	46	51	71	45	28	60	51	52	58	64
Manslaughter & infanticide	50	89	100	50	109	43	200	160	75	100
Attempted murder	24	20	46	24	28	27	34	35	31	74
Other violence against the person	47	66	71	61	65	66	67	65	69	67
SEXUAL OFFENCES	79	91	84	85	92	87	80	74	89	82
Rape	78	88	74	90	88	80	80	76	69	83
Attempted rape	78	80	50	67	77	97	71	81	73	70
Incest	100	94	103	92	89	84	106	80	71	115
Indecent assault	72	85	84	82	89	83	73	80	82	81
Other sexual offences	82	100	88	89	100	94	90	63	112	82
BURGLARY	26	30	29	27	22	22	19	20	20	19
Burglary in a dwelling	21	27	25	23	20	18	16	15	16	18
Burglary in a building other than a dwelling	25	28	27	28	22	21	19	22	22	19
Other burglary [1]	52	62	62	54	44	54	46	43	43	98
ROBBERY	19	19	23	22	18	17	19	15	20	19
Armed robbery	16	20	22	24	20	18	17	14	18	17
Hijacking	25	14	23	17	13	9	24	13	22	10
Other robbery	18	21	23	26	19	21	19	18	21	27
THEFT	38	43	45	43	36	34	32	34	31	31
Theft from the person	15	21	25	26	23	24	17	19	16	15
Theft in a dwelling	51	53	62	61	65	54	57	66	63	57
Theft from motor vehicles	14	18	22	21	14	12	9	10	8	10
Shoplifting	84	91	100	88	89	92	85	83	86	83
Theft or unauthorised taking of motor vehicles	34	39	46	46	31	29	27	30	19	18
Other thefts	31	36	36	37	31	31	29	31	30	28
FRAUD & FORGERY	71	79	84	79	74	67	61	62	65	63
Frauds	71	80	84	78	74	68	43	64	71	66
Forgery	67	78	84	87	77	52	63	45	38	39
CRIMINAL DAMAGE	31	43	41	34	36	32	33	35	36	33
Arson	23	30	25	24	22	20	22	19	20	18
Explosives offences	39	32	38	31	37	33	12	31	26	62
Other criminal damage [2]	35	51	51	40	43	38	41	43	43	39
OFFENCES AGAINST THE STATE	73	72	86	81	84	77	80	77	81	90
Offences under the NI Emergency Provisions Act	96	101	102	95	97	101	97	95	90	167
Firearms offences	68	81	84	79	84	73	79	66	59	52
Other offences against the state	69	63	82	75	78	67	75	74	86	91
OTHER NOTIFIABLE OFFENCES	87	75	80	76	72	82	85	85	90	93
Drug offences [3]	*	*	*	*	*	99	92	91	93	94
Other notifiable offences	87	75	80	76	72	47	58	57	70	74
GRAND TOTAL	37	43	45	43	38	36	34	36	36	36

Notes: (1) From 1995 excludes 'Attempted burglary' which is included in 'Burglary in a dwelling' or 'Burglary in a building other than a dwelling'.

(2) Other criminal damage excludes offences where damage was under £200.

(3) Drug offences not available separately prior to 1991 - included in Other notifiable offences.

4. Court Proceedings

4.1 Most persons suspected by the police of having committed an offence are prosecuted. This chapter considers the number of defendants proceeded against at certain stages of the criminal justice process.

4.2 Proceedings in the criminal courts start in a court of summary jurisdiction. Adults appear in a Magistrates' Court where less serious cases are dealt with by way of summary hearing or trial. More serious cases are committed for trial to the Crown Court, if the Magistrate is satisfied there is a case to answer. Juveniles aged 10-16 normally appear first in a special juvenile court of summary jurisdiction, which is empowered to deal with a wider range of offences than the corresponding adult court. Further details of the operation of criminal courts in Northern Ireland are given in Appendix 2.

4.3 The statistics are based on returns made by the RUC on those defendants against whom proceedings were completed in the appropriate year. Although care is taken in completing and analysing the returns, the detail collected is subject to the inaccuracies inherent in any large scale recording system, and to variation in recording practice over time. The coverage is restricted to those prosecutions in which the RUC is involved, excluding prosecutions brought by certain government departments, public bodies and private individuals.

4.4 Offences are referred to as either indictable, summary or "triable-either-way" essentially depending on whether the case against an adult defendant must be heard at the Crown Court, Magistrates' Court, or under certain circumstances may be heard at either. For convenience all triable-either-way offences are now included under the heading 'indictable', irrespective of how the case was dealt with. In respect of years prior to 1986, some triable-either-way offences were counted as summary if dealt with in a Magistrates' Court. The scope and categorisation of offences referred to as indictable are explained in Appendix 1 and under "triable-either-way" offences in Appendix 2.

4.5 Offences can be further classified as scheduled or non-scheduled depending on whether or not they are included in Schedule 1 of the Northern Ireland (Emergency Provisions) Act 1991. Scheduled offences are those typically committed by terrorists. In the Crown Court scheduled offences are dealt with in special non jury courts. The Attorney General has the power to "de-schedule" offences appearing in Schedule 1 where there was no act of terrorism involved e.g. a domestic murder. These and non-scheduled offences are processed through the normal Crown Court jury system. The Attorney General also has the power to certify certain scheduled offences as being suitable for summary trial in Magistrates' Courts. The most significant example is the offence of Assault Occasioning Actual Bodily Harm (AOABH). The statistics of scheduled offences in this chapter refer only to those heard in Crown Courts.

4.6 The offence shown in the tables is one for which the court took its final decision. This is not necessarily the same as that for which the defendant was initially proceeded against. The decision recorded is that reached by the court and takes no account of any subsequent appeal to a higher court. If a number of defendants are jointly charged with a particular offence, each is recorded, as will be any charges dealt with on separate occasions. Where proceedings involve more than one offence dealt with at the same time, the tables record only the principal offence. The basis for selection of the principal offence is laid down in rules issued by the Home Office. In summary these indicate that, where there is a finding of guilt, the principal offence is usually that for which the greatest penalty was imposed. Where there has not been a finding of guilt (e.g. on acquittal or committal for trial on all charges) it is usually that for which the greatest penalty could have been imposed.

4.7 Most proceedings are against individuals, but a few are against companies. Because the numbers are small they have not been shown separately and by convention are included with figures for adult males.

| *Magistrates' Courts* |

4.8 In 1995 the number of defendants proceeded against at Magistrates' Courts was 36,659, a 3% decrease on 1994. Total prosecutions for summary and indictable offences increased to a total of 15,035, up 2% on the previous year. Motoring prosecutions decreased in 1995 by 6% since 1994 to 21,624. Over the years a sizeable majority of all those proceeded against in Magistrates' Courts have been adult males (87% in 1995). In 1995, 31,741 adult males were proceeded against compared with 3,770 adult females, 1,041 male juveniles and 107 female juveniles. The number of juveniles proceeded against rose for the third consecutive year, but overall has fallen by 35% since 1986.

**Figure 4.1: DEFENDANTS PROCEEDED AGAINST AT MAGISTRATES'
COURTS 1986-1995**

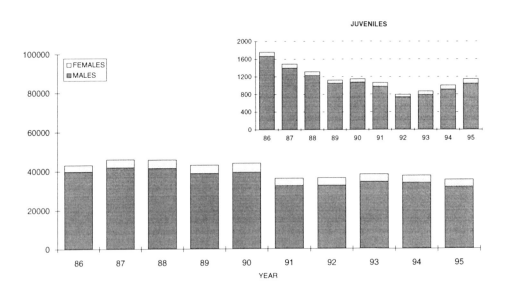

4.9 The type of offences with which adults and juveniles are proceeded against show a marked difference (see Figure 4.2). In the case of adults 61% of principal offences were motoring, 26% indictable, and 14% summary. In contrast 74% of the principal offences for juveniles were indictable, 19% summary, and 7% motoring. Offences of dishonesty (burglary, theft and fraud & forgery) accounted for the substantial majority of indictable offences - for adult offenders (51%) and juveniles (68%) and 53% overall.

Figure 4.2: MAGISTRATES' COURTS (Adults and Juveniles Proceeded Against) 1995

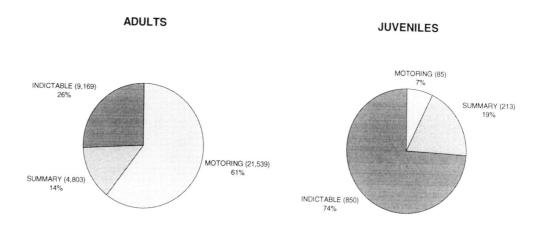

Percentages may not sum to 100% due to rounding.

Figure 4.3: MAGISTRATES' COURTS (Indictable Proceedings, Adults and Juveniles) 1995

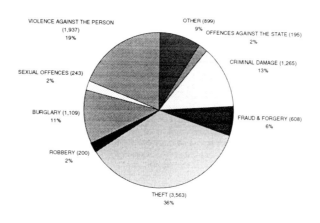

4.10 There were 1,249 defendants proceeded against in the Crown Court in 1995, the first annual increase since 1990 (1,422) and 3% higher than 1994. The vast majority 1,131 (91%) were adult males; of the remainder 87 were adult females, 31 were male juveniles and none were female juveniles. The 420 persons proceeded against for scheduled offences was up 5% on the previous year. The level of defendants being proceeded against for non-scheduled offences fell from 1,263 in 1986 to 818 in 1994 but rose by 1% to 829 in 1995, a fall of 34% on the 1986 figure.

Figure 4.4: DEFENDANTS PROCEEDED AGAINST AT THE CROWN COURT 1986-1995

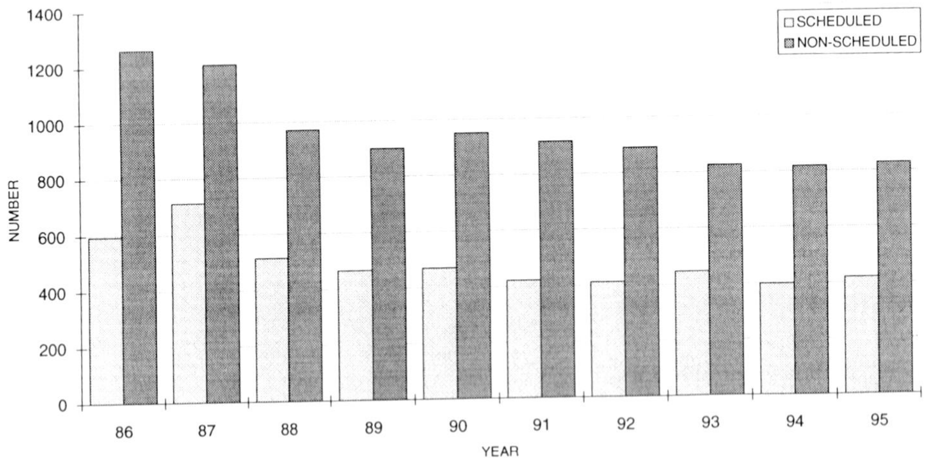

4.11 In a substantial majority of cases defendants plead guilty, whether in Magistrates' Court or the Crown Court, and whether charged with indictable, summary or motoring offences. In 1995 88% of defendants at the Magistrates' Court and 86% of defendants at the Crown pleaded guilty and as a consequence most cases resulted in a guilty finding. In Magistrates' Courts in 1995, 16% of defendants were found not guilty of indictable offences, 18% not guilty of summary offences and 7% not guilty of motoring offences. In the Crown Court 7% of defendants were acquitted.

4.12 However, of those pleading not guilty a sizeable proportion are acquitted of all charges. Overall in the Magistrates' Courts in 1995 of 4,364 pleading not guilty, 3,854 (88%) were acquitted. In the Crown Court of the 172 pleading not guilty, 92 (53%) were acquitted.

Figure 4.5: PLEAS AND FINDINGS FOR PRINCIPAL OFFENCES 1995

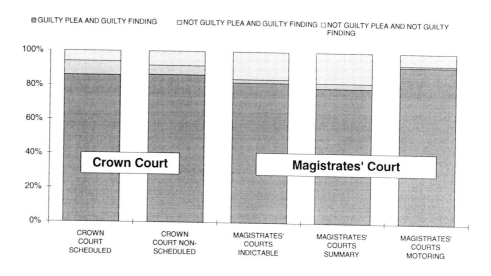

4.13 The number of offenders found guilty in relation to the population is shown in Figures 4.6 - 4.7 and in Table 4.11. Because a person found guilty on two or more separate occasions during the year is counted more than once, the rates shown over-estimate the proportion of the population who are known offenders in any one year. Overall the rate of conviction in 1995 was 237 per 10,000 population. The rate for females, at 47 per 10,000, is considerably less than that for males at 440 per 10,000. In 1995 the rate of conviction was highest for males aged 19 years and females aged 19 years.

Figure 4.6: RATE OF CONVICTION BY AGE AND SEX 1995

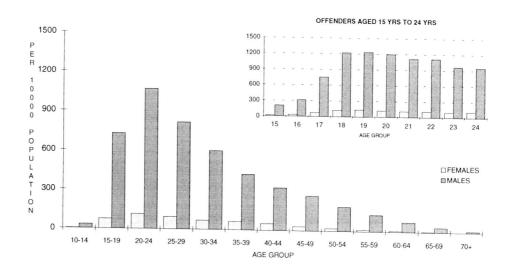

Figure 4.7: RATE OF CONVICTION FOR MALES BY AGE AND OFFENCE GROUP 1995

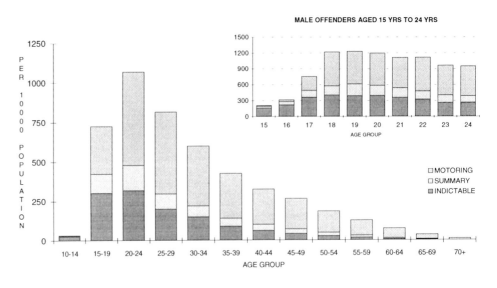

Juveniles

4.14 In 1995 there were 1,009 juveniles found guilty by the courts in Northern Ireland, 130 (15%) more than in 1994. This is the third consecutive annual increase. The percentage of juveniles found not guilty after pleading not guilty at the Magistrates' Court in 1995, was 90% for indictable offences, 87% for summary offences and 100% for motoring offences. Only one juvenile pleaded not guilty at the Crown Court in 1995. This juvenile was found guilty.

Previous Convictions

4.15 Of all those found guilty in 1995 (excluding companies and public bodies) 58% had previous convictions and the percentage is higher for males (60%) than females (35%). Figure 4.8 shows that previous convictions are more likely for persons convicted at the Crown Court than for those convicted at Magistrates' Courts.

Figure 4.8: PERCENTAGE OF THOSE FOUND GUILTY HAVING PREVIOUS CONVICTION(S) 1995

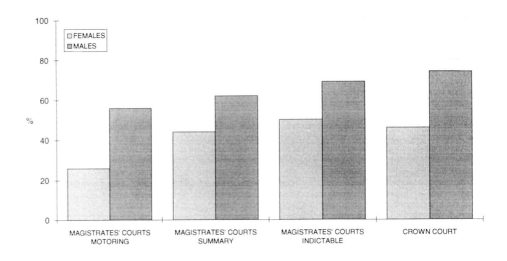

28

TABLE 4.1: Magistrates' Courts: Persons proceeded against by principal offence and sex (Adults and Juveniles) 1986-1995

CRIME CATEGORY		1986	1987	1988	1989	1990	1991	1992	1993	1994	1995
Violence against the person	Male	1362	1485	1512	1509	1856	1735	1658	1690	1568	1790
	Female	109	106	106	132	162	136	143	142	129	147
Sexual offences	Male	174	192	246	248	291	213	189	136	173	241
	Female	1	4	1	3	0	3	1	2	1	2
Burglary	Male	2019	1861	1592	1421	1433	1279	1267	1286	1087	1070
	Female	30	31	29	19	29	34	32	24	31	39
Robbery	Male	253	261	286	248	189	156	184	177	131	192
	Female	2	1	2	3	11	2	4	2	3	8
Theft	Male	3666	3583	3171	2971	3036	2981	2860	2967	2839	2907
	Female	778	867	745	664	770	810	696	712	659	656
Fraud and forgery	Male	570	584	581	635	586	514	564	569	500	479
	Female	124	133	148	194	154	170	167	146	114	129
Criminal damage	Male	1111	1221	1104	972	1161	1177	1011	1281	1301	1177
	Female	30	47	46	67	51	51	66	96	86	88
Offences against the state	Male	224	292	265	243	287	205	197	187	163	185
	Female	9	11	16	10	23	17	22	19	10	10
Other offences	Male	358	308	400	346	271	346	447	560	648	839
	Female	23	29	26	51	17	18	28	40	46	60
TOTAL INDICTABLE OFFENCES	Male	9737	9787	9157	8593	9110	8606	8377	8853	8410	8880
	Female	1106	1229	1119	1143	1217	1241	1159	1183	1079	1139
	TOTAL	10843	11016	10276	9736	10327	9847	9536	10036	9489	10019
SUMMARY OFFENCES [1]	Male	6472	6598	6442	5566	4653	4481	4211	4385	4727	4511
	Female	455	647	652	599	515	504	546	541	525	505
	TOTAL	6927	7245	7094	6165	5168	4985	4757	4926	5252	5016
MOTORING OFFENCES [2]	Male	25248	26873	27072	24707	25607	19329	19992	21221	20836	19391
	Female	1836	2470	2783	2613	3004	2063	2165	2270	2090	2233
	TOTAL	27084	29343	29855	27320	28611	21392	22157	23491	22926	21624
TOTAL NUMBER OF PERSONS PROCEEDED AGAINST		44854	47604	47225	43221	44106	36224	36450	38453	37667	36659

Notes: (1) Excluding motoring offences. From January 1986 this category excludes triable-each-way offences.
(2) Indictable and Summary motoring offences.

TABLE 4.2: Magistrates' Courts: Outcome for principal offence by plea and finding (Adults and Juveniles) 1986-1995

CRIME CATEGORY		1986	1987	1988	1989	1990	1991	1992	1993	1994	1995
INDICTABLE OFFENCES											
Persons proceeded against		10843	11016	10276	9736	10327	9847	9536	10036	9489	10019
Number of findings		9386	9686	9116	8497	9147	8711	8571	9133	8702	9048
PLEA:	not guilty	1097	1237	1205	1036	1323	1321	1502	1603	1539	1654
	guilty	8289	8449	7911	7461	7824	7390	7069	7530	7163	7394
FINDING:	not guilty	820	851	895	809	1083	1027	1148	1335	1384	1472
	guilty	8566	8835	8221	7688	8064	7684	7423	7798	7318	7576
% Not guilty pleas		12	13	13	12	14	15	18	18	18	18
% Not guilty findings		9	9	10	10	12	12	13	15	16	16
% Not guilty pleas resulting in not guilty findings		75	69	74	78	82	78	76	83	90	89
SUMMARY OFFENCES											
Persons proceeded against		6927	7245	7094	6165	5168	4985	4757	4926	5252	5016
Number of findings		6927	7245	7094	6165	5168	4985	4756	4926	5252	5016
PLEA:	not guilty	1330	1663	1534	1286	1065	884	953	828	1025	1020
	guilty	5597	5582	5560	4879	4103	4101	3803	4098	4227	3996
FINDING:	not guilty	834	1173	1023	1052	875	708	642	624	886	879
	guilty	6093	6072	6071	5113	4293	4277	4114	4302	4366	4137
% Not guilty pleas		19	23	22	21	21	18	20	17	20	20
% Not guilty findings		12	16	14	17	17	14	14	13	17	18
% Not guilty pleas resulting in not guilty findings		63	71	67	82	82	80	67	75	86	86
MOTORING OFFENCES											
Persons proceeded against		27084	29343	29855	27320	28611	21392	22157	23491	22926	21624
Number of findings		27076	29336	29847	27307	28590	21368	22146	23477	22919	21605
PLEA:	not guilty	1823	1898	1960	1684	1902	1671	2213	2122	1776	1690
	guilty	25253	27438	27887	25623	26688	19697	19933	21355	21143	19915
FINDING:	not guilty	1066	1136	1294	1211	1383	1235	1359	1615	1445	1503
	guilty	26010	28200	28553	26096	27207	20133	20787	21862	21474	20102
% Not guilty pleas		7	6	7	6	7	8	10	9	8	8
% Not guilty findings		4	4	4	4	5	6	6	7	6	7
% Not guilty pleas resulting in not guilty findings		58	60	66	72	73	74	61	76	81	89

TABLE 4.3: Magistrates' Courts: Juveniles proceeded against by principal offence and sex 1986-1995

CRIME CATEGORY		1986	1987	1988	1989	1990	1991	1992	1993	1994	1995
Violence against the person	Male	47	49	58	35	39	42	44	32	41	50
	Female	3	3	4	5	8	2	7	14	12	11
Sexual offences	Male	20	14	15	16	18	17	10	11	8	15
	Female	0	0	0	0	0	0	0	0	0	0
Burglary	Male	387	268	263	232	241	201	177	168	197	173
	Female	3	7	4	3	1	3	1	1	7	11
Robbery	Male	18	9	19	15	11	8	4	5	13	26
	Female	0	0	1	0	2	0	0	1	0	1
Theft	Male	510	405	397	299	315	303	232	291	276	332
	Female	49	50	56	31	38	53	35	31	42	43
Fraud and forgery	Male	9	24	7	14	10	10	16	14	14	14
	Female	1	1	0	1	0	3	1	3	2	8
Criminal damage	Male	161	182	126	128	98	107	81	101	138	132
	Female	4	6	3	4	2	2	2	9	8	7
Offences against the state	Male	10	19	19	14	8	5	6	2	10	12
	Female	0	2	2	0	0	0	0	0	0	0
Other offences	Male	11	8	11	9	10	9	9	3	6	15
	Female	0	0	0	2	1	0	0	0	0	0
TOTAL INDICTABLE OFFENCES	Male	1173	978	915	762	750	702	579	627	703	769
	Female	60	69	70	46	52	63	46	59	71	81
	TOTAL	1233	1047	985	808	802	765	625	686	774	850
SUMMARY OFFENCES [1]	Male	341	281	200	201	153	107	117	113	128	189
	Female	30	24	22	24	17	19	11	21	24	24
	TOTAL	371	305	222	225	170	126	128	134	152	213
MOTORING OFFENCES [2]	Male	150	137	108	86	95	66	44	50	78	83
	Female	5	2	2	2	5	6	1	2	3	2
	TOTAL	155	139	110	88	100	72	45	52	81	85
TOTAL NUMBER OF PERSONS PROCEEDED AGAINST		1759	1491	1317	1121	1072	963	798	872	1007	1148

Notes: (1) Excluding motoring offences. From January 1986 this category excludes triable-each-way offences.
(2) Indictable and Summary motoring offences.

TABLE 4.4: Magistrates' Courts: Outcome for principal offence by plea and finding for Juveniles 1986-1995

CRIME CATEGORY		1986	1987	1988	1989	1990	1991	1992	1993	1994	1995
INDICTABLE OFFENCES											
Juveniles proceeded against		1235	1047	985	808	802	765	625	686	774	850
Number of findings		1159	1024	956	771	771	728	605	672	753	822
PLEA:	not guilty	91	105	74	60	60	76	76	104	102	109
	guilty	1068	919	882	711	712	652	529	568	651	713
FINDING:	not guilty	78	81	65	54	45	66	51	86	98	98
	guilty	1081	943	891	717	726	662	554	586	655	724
% Not guilty pleas		8	10	8	8	8	10	13	15	14	13
% Not guilty findings		7	8	7	7	6	9	8	13	13	12
% Not guilty pleas resulting in not guilty findings		86	77	88	90	76	87	67	83	96	90
SUMMARY OFFENCES											
Juveniles proceeded against		371	305	222	225	170	126	128	134	152	211
Number of findings		371	305	222	225	170	126	128	134	152	21.
PLEA:	not guilty	80	69	43	43	36	20	26	12	23	3.
	guilty	291	236	179	182	134	106	102	122	129	17.
FINDING:	not guilty	58	43	32	39	32	15	15	9	21	3
	guilty	313	262	190	186	138	111	113	125	131	18
% Not guilty pleas		22	23	19	19	21	16	20	9	15	1
% Not guilty findings		16	14	14	17	19	12	12	7	14	1
% Not guilty pleas resulting in not guilty findings		73	62	74	91	89	75	58	75	91	8
MOTORING OFFENCES											
Juveniles proceeded against		155	139	110	88	100	72	45	52	81	8
Number of findings		155	139	110	88	99	72	45	51	81	8
PLEA:	not guilty	15	14	11	8	14	4	6	7	8	3
	guilty	140	125	99	80	85	68	39	44	73	
FINDING:	not guilty	12	11	10	7	8	1	5	7	8	
	guilty	143	128	100	81	91	71	40	44	73	
% Not guilty pleas		10	10	10	9	14	6	13	14	10	
% Not guilty findings		8	8	9	8	8	1	11	14	10	
% Not guilty pleas resulting in not guilty findings		80	79	91	88	57	25	83	100	100	1

TABLE 4.5: The Crown Court: Persons proceeded against by principal offence and sex (Adults and Juveniles) 1986-1995

CRIME CATEGORY		1986	1987	1988	1989	1990	1991	1992	1993	1994	1995
Violence against the person	Male	321	365	300	291	394	373	311	404	352	324
	Female	10	12	18	25	23	28	22	24	29	18
Sexual offences	Male	126	138	102	114	129	107	104	75	80	96
	Female	0	4	1	1	0	1	1	1	1	3
Burglary	Male	427	325	181	129	97	133	121	116	91	57
	Female	10	3	0	0	5	4	3	1	3	2
Robbery	Male	314	319	290	280	212	154	210	157	166	180
	Female	5	2	1	5	7	7	4	2	3	7
Theft	Male	214	192	184	134	141	172	169	143	160	151
	Female	27	32	36	28	45	36	32	40	29	21
Fraud and forgery	Male	64	96	69	89	79	58	52	33	41	44
	Female	8	11	13	15	6	10	14	7	7	11
Criminal damage	Male	182	230	135	91	92	64	89	66	73	68
	Female	2	3	2	7	4	4	7	7	5	5
Offences against the state	Male	66	103	41	56	70	66	78	66	41	58
	Female	11	9	3	14	13	10	11	11	2	1
Other offences [1]	Male	72	75	103	83	99	105	69	111	120	184
	Female	0	4	7	5	6	10	7	9	14	19
	Male	1786	1843	1405	1267	1313	1232	1203	1171	1124	1162
	Female	73	80	81	100	109	110	101	102	93	87
	TOTAL	**1859**	**1923**	**1486**	**1367**	**1422**	**1342**	**1304**	**1273**	**1217**	**1249**

Notes: (1) Includes Motoring Offences.

TABLE 4.6: The Crown Court: Persons proceeded against by offence group; scheduled and non-scheduled offences (Adults and Juveniles) 1986-1995

OFFENCE GROUP	1986	1987	1988	1989	1990	1991	1992	1993	1994	1995
Scheduled	596	713	515	456	470	423	413	447	399	420
Non-scheduled	1263	1210	971	911	952	919	891	826	818	829
TOTAL	**1859**	**1923**	**1486**	**1367**	**1422**	**1342**	**1304**	**1273**	**1217**	**1249**

TABLE 4.7: The Crown Court: Outcome for principal offence by plea and finding (Adults and Juveniles) 1986-1995

		1986	1987	1988	1989	1990	1991	1992	1993	1994	1995
Persons proceeded against		1859	1923	1486	1367	1422	1342	1304	1273	1217	1249
PLEA:	not guilty	230	233	261	227	320	282	330	361	283	172
	guilty	1629	1690	1225	1140	1102	1060	974	912	934	1077
FINDING:	not guilty	113	108	119	133	166	133	169	151	159	92
	guilty	1746	1815	1367	1234	1256	1209	1135	1122	1058	1157
% Not guilty pleas		12	12	18	17	23	21	25	28	23	14
% Not guilty findings		6	6	8	10	12	10	13	12	13	7
% Not guilty pleas resulting in not guilty findings		49	46	46	59	52	47	51	42	56	53

TABLE 4.8: The Crown Court: Juveniles proceeded against by principal offence and finding 1986-1995

CRIME CATEGORY		1986	1987	1988	1989	1990	1991	1992	1993	1994	1995
Violence against the person		7	8	5	4	6	3	6	4	10	2
Sexual offences		5	2	1	3	4	4	2	1	3	0
Burglary		29	14	4	6	0	12	6	5	4	4
Robbery		12	7	7	6	6	5	7	2	2	8
Theft		11	2	4	4	2	4	4	0	4	5
Fraud and forgery		1	0	0	0	0	0	0	0	0	0
Criminal damage		13	9	3	6	9	8	14	2	0	11
Offences against the state		0	1	2	3	0	0	0	0	0	1
Other offences		0	2	0	4	2	2	0	0	1	0
TOTAL		**78**	**45**	**26**	**36**	**29**	**38**	**39**	**14**	**24**	**31**
of which:	Male	77	45	26	34	28	34	36	14	19	31
	Female	1	0	0	2	1	4	3	0	5	0
PLEA	not guilty	8	7	6	1	8	8	8	4	6	1
	guilty	70	38	20	35	21	30	31	10	18	30
FINDING	not guilty	2	4	5	1	6	7	4	0	4	0
	guilty	76	41	21	35	23	31	35	14	20	31

TABLE 4.9: Scheduled Offences: Persons proceeded against by principal offence and finding (Adults and Juveniles) 1986-1995

CRIME CATEGORY		1986	1987	1988	1989	1990	1991	1992	1993	1994	1995
Violence against the person		178	190	156	139	181	179	130	204	134	148
Burglary		9	2	4	7	9	4	10	6	23	2
Robbery		209	244	226	188	143	97	149	116	136	135
Theft		0	0	0	0	0	0	0	0	11	7
Fraud and forgery		0	0	0	0	0	0	0	0	3	1
Criminal damage		120	173	76	53	51	28	28	28	38	26
Offences against the state		65	100	40	59	69	74	80	71	37	45
Other offences		15	4	13	10	17	41	16	22	17	56
TOTAL		**596**	**713**	**515**	**456**	**470**	**423**	**413**	**447**	**399**	**420**
of which:	Male	574	694	503	428	445	390	385	425	385	399
	Female	22	19	12	28	25	33	28	22	14	21
PLEA	not guilty	68	79	73	83	84	80	112	119	80	60
	guilty	528	634	442	373	386	343	301	328	319	360
FINDING	not guilty	29	33	28	42	30	35	59	34	35	23
	guilty	567	680	487	414	440	388	354	413	364	397

TABLE 4.10: Scheduled Offences: Juveniles proceeded against by principal offence and finding 1986-1995

CRIME CATEGORY		1986	1987	1988	1989	1990	1991	1992	1993	1994	1995
Violence against the person		5	2	2	1	4	0	0	0	1	0
Burglary		0	0	0	1	0	0	0	1	1	0
Robbery		8	3	4	3	1	4	6	2	2	5
Theft		0	0	0	0	0	0	0	0	0	1
Criminal damage		7	3	3	3	4	2	3	1	0	0
Offences against the state		0	1	2	2	0	0	0	0	0	0
TOTAL		**20**	**9**	**11**	**10**	**9**	**6**	**9**	**4**	**4**	**6**
of which:	Male	20	9	11	9	9	4	9	4	3	6
	Female	0	0	0	1	0	2	0	0	1	0
PLEA	not guilty	0	0	1	0	1	2	1	0	0	1
	guilty	20	9	10	10	8	4	8	4	4	5
FINDING	not guilty	0	0	1	0	1	2	1	0	0	0
	guilty	20	9	10	10	8	4	8	4	4	6

TABLE 4.11: Persons found guilty (All Courts) by age and sex 1995 and rates per 10,000 population

	AGE GROUP	NUMBER OF PERSONS IN AGE GROUP				NUMBER PER 10,000 POPULATION			
		INDICTABLE	SUMMARY	MOTORING	TOTAL	INDICTABLE	SUMMARY	MOTORING	TOTAL
MALE	10-14	180	31	6	217	27	5	1	32
	15-19	1931	777	1939	4647	302	121	303	726
	20-24	2122	1057	3926	7105	319	159	590	1068
	25-29	1270	616	3305	5191	200	97	520	816
	30-34	918	430	2343	3691	149	70	381	601
	35-39	496	284	1594	2374	89	51	286	426
	40-44	307	188	1122	1617	62	38	226	326
	45-49	201	139	941	1281	42	29	195	266
	50-54	119	92	593	804	28	21	137	186
	55-59	61	51	357	469	17	14	97	128
	60-64	25	19	199	243	8	6	61	75
	65-69	13	12	81	106	4	4	28	36
	70+	2	6	58	66	0	1	11	12
	Unknown	67	62	1632	1761				
FEMALE	10-14	16	2	0	18	2	0	0	3
	15-19	237	69	146	452	39	11	24	75
	20-24	233	63	396	692	38	10	65	113
	25-29	145	66	383	594	23	10	60	93
	30-34	128	58	258	444	20	9	40	69
	35-39	82	50	230	362	14	9	40	63
	40-44	65	22	164	251	13	4	33	51
	45-49	44	12	109	165	9	2	22	33
	50-54	17	9	67	93	4	2	15	21
	55-59	15	8	33	56	4	2	8	14
	60-64	4	3	22	29	1	1	6	8
	65-69	4	1	9	14	1	0	3	4
	70+	1	1	5	7	0	0	1	1
	Unknown	8	9	206	223				
MALES		7712	3764	18096	29572	115	56	269	440
FEMALES		999	373	2028	3400	14	5	28	47
TOTAL		8711	4137	20124	32972	63	30	145	237

TABLE 4.12: Percentage of persons found guilty having previous conviction(s) (Adults and Juveniles) 1986-1995

	1986	1987	1988	1989	1990	1991	1992	1993	1994	1995
MALE										
The Crown Court	49	69	77	75	76	80	80	79	80	74
Magistrates' Court - Indictable Offences	40	62	65	65	59	73	70	69	69	69
Magistrates' Court - Summary Offences	41	54	62	62	61	70	67	66	67	62
Magistrates' Court - Motoring Offences	34	50	52	54	55	56	55	54	56	56
FEMALE										
The Crown Court	33	43	22	27	50	40	47	41	54	46
Magistrates' Court - Indictable Offences	22	35	36	36	34	46	46	47	51	50
Magistrates' Court - Summary Offences	28	38	36	39	43	46	42	42	45	44
Magistrates' Court - Motoring Offences	12	17	17	19	18	20	21	22	26	26

5. Sentencing

Introduction

5.1 This chapter deals with persons convicted and sentenced in Northern Ireland courts. Analysis of sentencing is based on the most severe penalty imposed by the court for the principal offence. No account is taken of the outcome of any subsequent appeal.

5.2 When sentencing convicted offenders, Judges and Magistrates can impose a variety of sanctions within the limits prescribed by Parliament. They can choose from a variety of options such as fines or discharges. They can decide on an amount of community supervision required for an offender as in the case of probation or community service orders, or they can consider some form of imprisonment. Appendix 3 summarises the main sentences available to the courts. In imposing sentences, Judges and Magistrates will take account of the characteristics of the offender such as age, previous convictions, financial and domestic circumstances, and characteristics of the offence in terms of seriousness and the degree of culpability.

5.3 Changes in the different types of sentence are not necessarily a reflection of changes in sentencing practice but may be due to variations in any of the factors referred to above. Trends in sentencing over time must therefore be interpreted with caution. A procedural change in the classification of all triable-either-way offences into the indictable category further confounds comparison of 1986 and subsequent data with that for earlier years. This chapter does however provide basic information on the demands made on those agencies which supervise convicted offenders such as prisons and probation. More specifically the chapter identifies and distinguishes the sentences imposed in the Magistrates' Court and the Crown Court for juveniles and adults. It further identifies in the Crown Court those individuals whose offences were scheduled i.e. listed in relevant schedules of the Northern Ireland (Emergency Provisions) Acts 1978-1991.

**Crown Court
Sentencing**

5.4 In total 1,157 persons were sentenced at the Crown Court during 1995, an increase of 9% since 1994. Of that total, 615 (53%) were sentenced to immediate custody, the same as the proportion sentenced to immediate custody in 1994. A further 328 (28%) received a suspended custodial sentence. In 1995 there were 60 community service orders and 60 probation orders representing 10% of all sentences given. In 1995, therefore, 10% of all those sentenced by the Crown Court were given supervision in the community - this is the lowest proportion recorded during the 1986-1995 period.

5.5 Immediate custodial sentences tend to be given more for scheduled offences than non-scheduled offences, and this continued to be the case in 1995 (see Figure 5.2). Of the 397 persons sentenced for scheduled offences in 1995, 66% received immediate custodial sentences. This is 1 percentage point less than in 1994. A further 24% received suspended custodial sentences and 7% supervision in the community. This compares with 46% being given immediate custody, 30% receiving suspended custody and 12% receiving supervision in the community for non-scheduled offences.

Figure 5.1: CROWN COURT SENTENCING: MAIN DISPOSALS 1986-1995

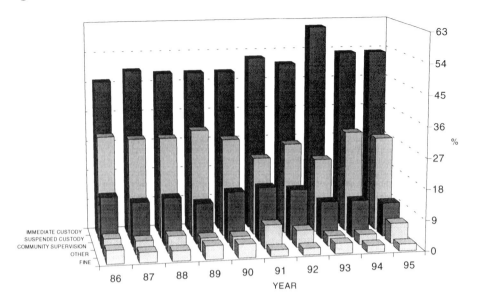

Figure 5.2: CROWN COURT SENTENCING 1995

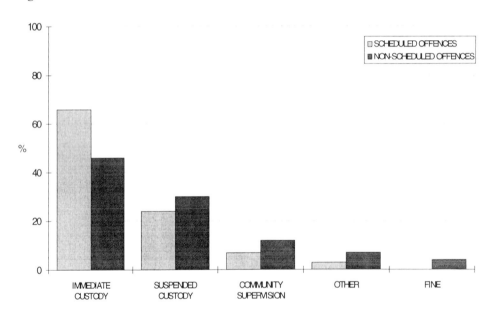

Magistrates' Courts

5.6 In 1995, 31,815 offenders were sentenced at Magistrates' Courts, of which 7,576 were for indictable offences, 4,137 for summary offences, and 20,102 for motoring offences. The number of motoring offenders, who make up 63% of those sentenced, decreased by 6% over the previous year, while the number sentenced for the combined indictable/summary categories increased marginally from 11,684 to 11,713.

5.7 Figures 5.3-5.5 show that for each category of offender the fine was by far the most common disposal. In 1995 71% of all offenders in Magistrates' Courts were fined. Fines were given for 29% of indictable offences, 49% of summary offences, and 92% of motoring offences. In relative terms immediate custodial sentences are less frequently used than in the Crown Court, reflecting the less serious nature of the offences dealt with. In 1995 immediate custodial disposals were given for 17% of indictable offences, 2% of summary offences and 1% of motoring offences. In total 1,698 offenders received sentences of immediate custody from the Magistrates' Courts. This figure was nearly three times the number of people given immediate custody sentences at the Crown Court. Comparing 1994 to 1995 the proportionate use of immediate custody in Magistrates' Courts was equal at 5% of all disposals. The proportion of fines in 1995 was 71% of all sentences, 3 percentage points lower than in 1994.

Figure 5.3: MAGISTRATES' COURTS (Sentencing: Indictable Offences) 1995

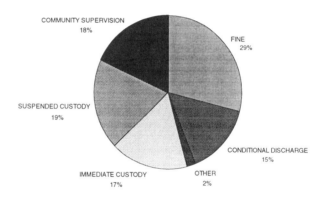

Percentages may not sum to 100% due to rounding

Figure 5.4: MAGISTRATES' COURTS (Sentencing: Summary Offences) 1995

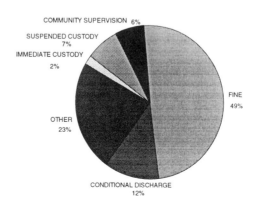

Percentages may not sum to 100% due to rounding

41

Figure 5.5: MAGISTRATES' COURTS (Sentencing: Motoring Offences) 1995

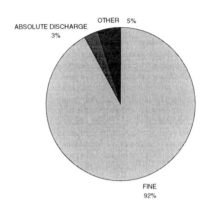

Percentages may not sum to 100% due to rounding

5.8 Figure 5.6 illustrates the annual proportions of the various disposals for indictable and summary offences in recent years. Fines have fallen from 46% of all disposals in 1986 to 36% in 1995.

Figure 5.6: MAGISTRATES' COURTS SENTENCING - MAIN DISPOSALS (Indictable and Summary Offences Only 1986-1995)

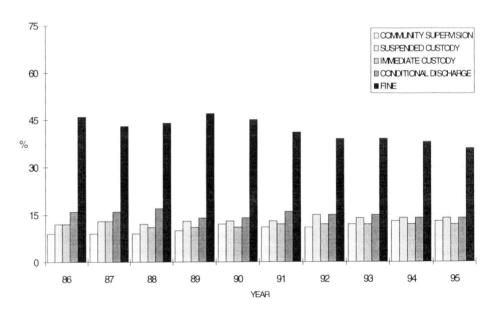

Juvenile Sentences

5.9 In 1995 there were 1,009 juveniles sentenced by the courts, 755 for indictable offences, 180 for summary offences, and 74 for motoring offences. 228 juveniles were sentenced to custodial supervision (most in the form of Training School Orders) in 1995 constituting 23% of all juvenile disposals. This rate shows a decrease of 2 percentage points from the 1994 rate of 25%. Figure 5.7 shows the relative use of various disposals for juveniles convicted of summary and indictable crime. Only a small number of motoring offences are committed by juveniles (taking and driving away is an offence of theft), so they have been excluded from this chart.

Figure 5.7: JUVENILE SENTENCING - MAIN DISPOSALS AT ALL COURTS
(Indictable and Summary Offences Only 1986-1995)

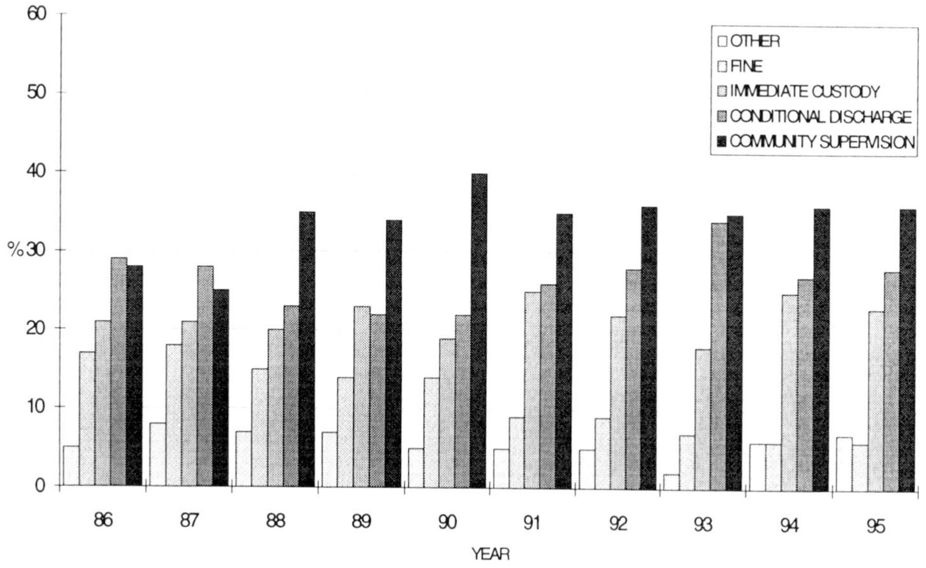

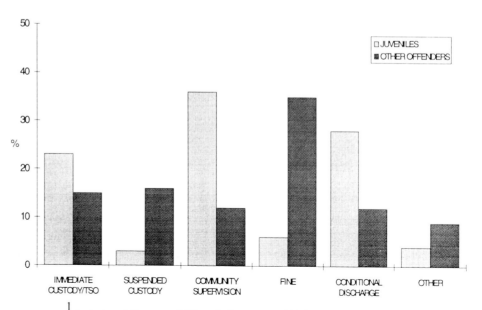

5.10 Disposals given to juveniles for indictable and summary offences by the courts vary from those given to other offenders, in part reflecting the different nature of offences of which juveniles are found guilty. Figure 5.8 compares the disposals given for indictable and summary offences to juveniles with those given to other offenders. Juveniles found guilty are more likely than other offenders to receive custodial supervision (again mainly Training School Orders), supervision in the community or a conditional discharge; but less likely to receive a suspended sentence or a fine.

Figure 5.8: ALL COURT DISPOSALS: JUVENILES AND OTHER[1] OFFENDERS
(Indictable and Summary Offences) 1995

[1] Includes all those aged 17+, missing ages, public bodies and companies

43

TABLE 5.1: Crown Court Sentencing (Adults and Juveniles) 1986-1995

SENTENCE   NUMBER OF PERSONS

	1986	1987	1988	1989	1990	1991	1992	1993	1994	1995
Prison	570	681	536	472	493	493	447	555	471	533
Young Offenders' Centre	216	199	112	111	106	125	119	130	87	76
Training School	19	16	5	10	4	13	5	2	5	6
Total Immediate Custody	805	896	653	593	603	631	571	687	563	615
Prison Suspended/Recorded	406	389	313	318	295	238	249	211	277	265
YOC Suspended/Recorded	145	172	93	73	78	46	63	37	43	63
Attendance Centre	0	0	1	2	0	0	0	0	1	0
Probation/Supervision	105	86	80	72	85	103	95	73	58	60
Community Service Order	150	141	106	71	105	89	79	48	59	60
Fine	46	50	35	39	33	23	17	33	23	27
Recognizance	9	14	7	3	8	7	9	5	16	0
Conditional Discharge	78	55	65	51	37	53	36	19	15	64
Absolute Discharge	3	3	5	1	2	5	8	3	2	1
Fine plus Disqualification	10	7	4	8	10	6	2	0	0	0
Other	7	2	5	3	0	8	6	6	1	2
All Sentences	1764	1815	1367	1234	1256	1209	1135	1122	1058	1157

PERCENTAGE OF ALL SENTENCES

	1986	1987	1988	1989	1990	1991	1992	1993	1994	1995
Prison	32	38	39	38	39	41	40	49	45	46
Young Offenders' Centre	12	11	8	9	8	10	10	12	8	7
Training School	1	1	0	1	0	1	0	0	0	1
Total Immediate Custody	46	49	48	48	48	52	50	61	53	53
Prison Suspended/Recorded	23	21	23	26	23	20	22	19	26	23
YOC Suspended/Recorded	8	9	7	6	6	4	6	3	4	5
Attendance Centre	0	0	0	0	0	0	0	0	0	0
Probation/Supervision	6	5	6	6	7	9	8	7	6	5
Community Service Order	9	8	8	6	8	7	7	4	6	5
Fine	3	3	3	3	3	2	1	3	2	2
Recognizance	1	1	1	0	1	1	1	0	2	0
Conditional Discharge	4	3	5	4	3	4	3	2	1	6
Absolute Discharge	0	0	0	0	0	0	1	0	0	0
Fine plus Disqualification	1	0	0	1	1	0	0	0	0	0
Other	0	0	0	0	0	1	1	1	0	0

Note: (1)   Percentage components may not sum to 100% due to rounding.

TABLE 5.2: Crown Court Sentencing: Scheduled offences (Adults and Juveniles) 1986-1995

SENTENCE

NUMBER OF PERSONS

	1986	1987	1988	1989	1990	1991	1992	1993	1994	1995
Prison	237	261	221	203	203	225	186	270	217	235
Young Offenders' Centre	92	81	44	34	53	48	36	39	26	26
Training School	4	1	4	1	0	0	1	0	1	1
Total Immediate Custody	333	343	269	238	256	273	223	309	244	262
Prison Suspended/Recorded	110	148	104	85	78	60	74	61	68	72
YOC Suspended/Recorded	61	107	43	37	42	15	30	19	11	25
Attendance Centre	0	0	0	0	0	0	0	0	1	0
Probation/Supervision	26	21	13	17	17	12	12	15	14	15
Community Service Order	19	32	41	21	39	23	8	4	16	11
Fine	5	10	2	0	0	0	0	1	0	0
Recognizance	2	1	2	0	1	1	1	0	8	0
Conditional Discharge	9	17	13	16	7	1	2	4	2	12
Absolute Discharge	1	1	0	0	0	1	4	0	0	0
Fine plus Disqualification	0	0	0	0	0	0	0	0	0	0
Other	1	0	0	0	0	2	0	0	0	0
All Sentences	567	680	487	414	440	388	354	413	364	397

PERCENTAGE OF ALL SENTENCES

	1986	1987	1988	1989	1990	1991	1992	1993	1994	1995
Prison	42	38	45	49	46	58	53	65	60	59
Young Offenders' Centre	16	12	9	8	12	12	10	9	7	7
Training School	1	0	1	0	0	0	0	0	0	0
Total Immediate Custody	59	50	55	57	58	70	63	75	67	66
Prison Suspended/Recorded	19	22	21	21	18	15	21	15	19	18
YOC Suspended/Recorded	11	16	9	9	10	4	8	5	3	6
Attendance Centre	0	0	0	0	0	0	0	0	0	0
Probation/Supervision	5	3	3	4	4	3	3	4	4	4
Community Service Order	3	5	8	5	9	6	2	1	4	3
Fine	1	1	0	0	0	0	0	0	0	0
Recognizance	0	0	0	0	0	0	0	0	2	0
Conditional Discharge	2	3	3	4	2	0	1	1	1	3
Absolute Discharge	0	0	0	0	0	0	1	0	0	0
Fine plus Disqualification	0	0	0	0	0	0	0	0	0	0
Other	0	0	0	0	0	1	0	0	0	0

Note: (1) Percentage components may not sum to 100% due to rounding.

TABLE 5.3: Magistrates' Courts Sentencing: Indictable offences (Adults and Juveniles) 1986-1995

SENTENCE

NUMBER OF PERSONS

	1986	1987	1988	1989	1990	1991	1992	1993	1994	1995
Prison	841	1031	891	767	747	724	618	764	672	763
Young Offenders' Centre	355	353	338	310	313	430	480	469	405	405
Training School	227	197	152	150	138	156	115	114	165	156
Total Immediate Custody	1423	1581	1381	1227	1198	1310	1213	1347	1242	1324
Prison Suspended/Recorded	1077	1324	1177	1130	1064	955	980	1036	1017	1103
YOC Suspended/Recorded	245	274	231	259	247	328	363	328	313	292
Attendance Centre	95	89	125	93	97	80	58	86	81	82
Probation/Supervision	678	584	666	648	727	648	708	718	772	890
Community Service Order	380	414	383	341	472	451	364	407	422	401
Fine	2786	2647	2528	2504	2704	2271	2267	2389	2180	2176
Recognizance	65	92	51	52	63	81	89	87	87	95
Conditional Discharge	1635	1662	1516	1294	1340	1429	1293	1345	1148	1166
Absolute Discharge	106	106	94	90	101	76	61	49	48	40
Fine plus Disqualification	64	57	51	42	39	40	20	0	0	0
Other	12	5	18	8	12	15	7	6	8	7
All Sentences	8566	8835	8221	7688	8064	7684	7423	7798	7318	7576

PERCENTAGE OF ALL SENTENCES

	1986	1987	1988	1989	1990	1991	1992	1993	1994	1995
Prison	10	12	11	10	9	9	8	10	9	10
Young Offenders' Centre	4	4	4	4	4	6	6	6	6	5
Training School	3	2	2	2	2	2	2	1	2	2
Total Immediate Custody	17	18	17	16	15	17	16	17	17	17
Prison Suspended/Recorded	13	15	14	15	13	12	13	13	14	15
YOC Suspended/Recorded	3	3	3	3	3	4	5	4	4	4
Attendance Centre	1	1	2	1	1	1	1	1	1	1
Probation/Supervision	8	7	8	8	9	8	10	9	11	12
Community Service Order	4	5	5	4	6	6	5	5	6	5
Fine	33	30	31	33	34	30	31	31	30	29
Recognizance	1	1	1	1	1	1	1	1	1	1
Conditional Discharge	19	19	18	17	17	19	17	17	16	15
Absolute Discharge	1	1	1	1	1	1	1	1	0	1
Fine plus Disqualification	1	1	1	1	0	1	0	0	0	0
Other	0	0	0	0	0	0	0	0	0	0

Note: (1) Percentage components may not sum to 100% due to rounding.

TABLE 5.4: Magistrates' Courts Sentencing: Summary offences (Adults and Juveniles) 1986-1995

SENTENCE

NUMBER OF PERSONS

	1986	1987	1988	1989	1990	1991	1992	1993	1994	1995
Prison	220	239	164	125	115	113	81	75	90	70
Young Offenders' Centre	94	67	36	33	27	48	55	38	21	21
Training School	29	17	12	13	9	6	5	8	13	8
Total Immediate Custody	343	323	212	171	151	167	141	121	124	99
Prison Suspended/Recorded	358	285	273	244	234	199	248	249	239	235
YOC Suspended/Recorded	92	89	53	42	47	73	89	60	70	42
Attendance Centre	6	14	12	13	12	6	5	6	5	11
Probation/Supervision	103	104	80	111	98	68	106	118	157	164
Community Service Order	71	78	103	65	72	64	61	67	66	75
Fine	3889	3818	3771	3498	2803	2692	2274	2352	2302	2040
Recognizance	353	500	386	357	334	428	620	769	872	905
Conditional Discharge	716	668	964	494	404	472	476	489	458	509
Absolute Discharge	157	185	204	110	123	105	90	70	71	56
Fine plus Disqualification	0	3	1	0	1	0	0	0	0	0
Other	5	5	12	8	14	3	4	1	2	1
All Sentences	6093	6072	6071	5113	4293	4277	4114	4302	4366	4137

PERCENTAGE OF ALL SENTENCES

	1986	1987	1988	1989	1990	1991	1992	1993	1994	1995
Prison	4	4	3	2	3	3	2	2	2	2
Young Offenders' Centre	2	1	1	1	1	1	1	1	1	1
Training School	0	0	0	0	0	0	0	0	0	0
Total Immediate Custody	6	5	3	3	4	4	3	3	3	2
Prison Suspended/Recorded	6	5	4	5	5	5	6	6	5	6
YOC Suspended/Recorded	2	1	1	1	1	2	2	1	2	1
Attendance Centre	0	0	0	0	0	0	0	0	0	0
Probation/Supervision	2	2	1	2	2	2	3	3	4	4
Community Service Order	1	1	2	1	2	1	1	2	2	2
Fine	64	63	62	68	65	63	55	55	53	49
Recognizance	6	8	6	7	8	10	15	18	20	22
Conditional Discharge	12	11	16	10	9	11	12	11	10	12
Absolute Discharge	3	3	3	2	3	2	2	2	2	1
Fine plus Disqualification	0	0	0	0	0	0	0	0	0	0
Other	0	0	0	0	0	0	0	0	0	0

Note: (1) Percentage components may not sum to 100% due to rounding.

TABLE 5.5: Magistrates' Courts Sentencing: Indictable and Summary offences (Adults and Juveniles) 1986-1995

SENTENCE   NUMBER OF PERSONS

	1986	1987	1988	1989	1990	1991	1992	1993	1994	1995
Prison	1061	1270	1055	892	862	837	699	839	762	833
Young Offenders' Centre	449	420	374	343	340	478	535	507	426	426
Training School	256	214	164	163	147	162	120	122	178	164
Total Immediate Custody	1766	1904	1593	1398	1349	1477	1354	1468	1366	1423
Prison Suspended/Recorded	1435	1609	1450	1374	1298	1154	1228	1285	1256	1338
YOC Suspended/Recorded	337	363	284	301	294	401	452	388	383	334
Attendance Centre	101	103	137	106	109	86	63	92	86	93
Probation/Supervision	781	688	746	759	825	716	814	836	929	1054
Community Service Order	451	492	486	406	544	515	425	474	488	476
Fine	6675	6465	6299	6002	5507	4963	4541	4741	4482	4216
Recognizance	418	592	437	409	397	509	709	856	959	1000
Conditional Discharge	2351	2330	2480	1788	1744	1901	1769	1834	1606	1675
Absolute Discharge	263	291	298	200	224	181	151	119	119	96
Fine plus Disqualification	64	60	52	42	40	40	20	0	0	0
Other	17	10	30	16	26	18	11	7	10	8
All Sentences	14659	14907	14292	12801	12357	11961	11537	12100	11684	11713

PERCENTAGE OF ALL SENTENCES

	1986	1987	1988	1989	1990	1991	1992	1993	1994	1995
Prison	7	9	7	7	7	7	6	7	7	7
Young Offenders' Centre	3	3	3	3	3	4	5	4	4	4
Training School	2	1	1	1	1	1	1	1	1	1
Total Immediate Custody	12	13	11	11	11	12	12	12	12	12
Prison Suspended/Recorded	10	11	10	11	11	10	11	11	11	11
YOC Suspended/Recorded	2	2	2	2	2	3	4	3	3	3
Attendance Centre	1	1	1	1	1	1	1	1	1	1
Probation/Supervision	5	5	5	6	7	6	7	7	8	9
Community Service Order	3	3	3	3	4	4	4	4	4	4
Fine	46	43	44	47	45	41	39	39	38	36
Recognizance	3	4	3	3	3	4	6	7	8	9
Conditional Discharge	16	16	17	14	14	16	15	15	14	14
Absolute Discharge	2	2	2	2	2	2	1	1	1	1
Fine plus Disqualification	0	0	0	0	0	0	0	0	0	0
Other	0	0	0	0	0	0	0	0	0	0

Note: (1)   Percentage components may not sum to 100% due to rounding.

TABLE 5.6: Magistrates' Courts Sentencing: Motoring offences (Adults and Juveniles) 1986-1995

SENTENCE   NUMBER OF PERSONS

	1986	1987	1988	1989	1990	1991	1992	1993	1994	1995
Prison	155	193	167	114	147	123	131	188	183	213
Young Offenders' Centre	21	32	27	25	30	24	53	68	73	57
Training School	8	6	6	5	6	15	0	3	15	5
Total Immediate Custody	184	231	200	144	183	162	184	259	271	275
Prison Suspended/Recorded	233	249	197	170	215	225	192	244	302	336
YOC Suspended/Recorded	21	23	26	18	16	31	55	59	64	51
Attendance Centre	3	4	2	2	9	4	3	2	3	8
Probation/Supervision	8	12	17	19	29	26	35	45	88	83
Community Service Order	25	27	37	29	31	32	39	62	63	71
Fine	19722	21309	21720	20304	21137	14606	18877	20425	19908	18510
Recognizance	3	8	5	3	2	5	4	2	2	1
Conditional Discharge	191	268	227	234	238	201	196	187	224	253
Absolute Discharge	1202	1366	1358	1105	1050	664	581	571	542	512
Fine plus Disqualification	4373	4674	4758	4064	4295	4171	620	6	6	2
Other	45	29	6	4	2	6	1	0	1	0
All Sentences	26010	28200	28553	26096	27207	20133	20787	21862	21474	20102

PERCENTAGE OF ALL SENTENCES

	1986	1987	1988	1989	1990	1991	1992	1993	1994	1995
Prison	1	1	1	0	1	1	1	1	1	1
Young Offenders' Centre	0	0	0	0	0	0	0	0	0	0
Training School	0	0	0	0	0	0	0	0	0	0
Total Immediate Custody	1	1	1	1	1	1	1	1	1	1
Prison Suspended/Recorded	1	1	1	1	1	1	1	1	1	2
YOC Suspended/Recorded	0	0	0	0	0	0	0	0	0	0
Attendance Centre	0	0	0	0	0	0	0	0	0	0
Probation/Supervision	0	0	0	0	0	0	0	0	0	0
Community Service Order	0	0	0	0	0	0	0	0	0	0
Fine	76	76	76	78	78	73	91	93	93	92
Recognizance	0	0	0	0	0	0	0	0	0	0
Conditional Discharge	1	1	1	1	1	1	1	1	1	1
Absolute Discharge	5	5	5	4	4	3	3	3	3	3
Fine plus Disqualification	17	17	17	16	16	21	3	0	0	0
Other	0	0	0	0	0	0	0	0	0	0

Note: (1)   Percentage components may not sum to 100% due to rounding.

TABLE 5.7: Disposals for each crime category at Magistrates' Courts and the Crown Court (Adults and Juveniles) 1995

CRIME CATEGORY	Immediate Custody	Suspended Custody	Supervision in the Community	Fine	Conditional Discharge	Other	TOTAL
MALE							
Violence against the person	327	380	137	517	150	44	1555
Sexual offences	75	37	38	11	16	1	178
Burglary	320	161	250	85	98	8	922
Robbery	119	43	20	0	4	0	186
Theft	528	492	547	636	340	19	2562
Fraud and forgery	59	114	61	123	55	1	413
Criminal damage	153	150	136	206	250	35	930
Offences against the state	32	51	12	42	20	4	161
Other offences	250	122	51	348	29	5	805
TOTAL INDICTABLE OFFENCES	1863	1550	1252	1968	962	117	7712
SUMMARY [1]	95	268	224	1918	431	828	3764
MOTORING [2]	279	387	159	16636	212	423	18096
ALL OFFENCES	2237	2205	1635	20522	1605	1368	29572
FEMALE							
Violence against the person	9	21	23	41	25	11	130
Sexual offences	3	0	1	0	0	0	4
Burglary	9	2	9	0	9	0	29
Robbery	1	2	3	0	3	0	9
Theft	27	95	150	121	163	10	566
Fraud and forgery	5	26	30	27	31	1	120
Criminal damage	11	7	18	12	24	6	78
Offences against the state	0	1	0	2	2	0	5
Other offences	6	8	6	28	10	0	58
TOTAL INDICTABLE OFFENCES	71	162	240	231	267	28	999
SUMMARY [1]	4	9	26	122	78	134	373
MOTORING [2]	1	11	4	1878	42	92	2028
ALL OFFENCES	76	182	270	2231	387	254	3400
TOTAL							
Violence against the person	336	401	160	558	175	55	1685
Sexual offences	78	37	39	11	16	1	182
Burglary	329	163	259	85	107	8	951
Robbery	120	45	23	0	7	0	195
Theft	555	587	697	757	503	29	3128
Fraud and forgery	64	140	91	150	86	2	533
Criminal damage	164	157	154	218	274	41	1008
Offences against the state	32	52	12	44	22	4	166
Other offences	256	130	57	376	39	5	863
TOTAL INDICTABLE OFFENCES	1934	1712	1492	2199	1229	145	8711
SUMMARY [1]	99	277	250	2040	509	962	4137
MOTORING [2]	280	398	163	18514	254	515	20124
ALL OFFENCES	2313	2387	1905	22753	1992	1622	32972

Note: (1) Excluding Motoring Offence.
(2) Indictable and Summary Motoring Offences.

TABLE 5.8: Percentage of disposals for each crime category at Magistrates' Courts and the Crown Court (Adults and Juveniles) 1995

CRIME CATEGORY	Immediate Custody	Suspended Custody	Supervision in the Community	Fine	Conditional Discharge	Other	TOTAL
Violence against the person	20	24	9	33	10	3	100
Sexual offences	43	20	21	6	9	1	100
Burglary	35	17	27	9	11	1	100
Robbery	62	23	12	0	4	0	100
Theft	18	19	22	24	16	1	100
Fraud and forgery	12	26	17	28	16	0	100
Criminal damage	16	16	15	22	27	4	100
Offences against the state	19	31	7	27	13	2	100
Other offences	30	15	7	44	5	1	100
TOTAL INDICTABLE OFFENCES	22	20	17	25	14	2	100
SUMMARY [1]	2	7	6	49	12	23	100
MOTORING [2]	1	2	1	92	1	3	100
ALL OFFENCES	7	7	6	69	6	5	100

Note: (1) Excluding Motoring Offence.
(2) Indictable and Summary Motoring Offences.
(3) Percentage components may not sum to 100% due to rounding.

TABLE 5.9: Juvenile disposals for each crime category at Magistrates' Courts and the Crown Court 1995

CRIME CATEGORY	Immediate Custody	Suspended Custody	Supervision in the Community	Fine	Conditional Discharge	Other	TOTAL
Violence against the person	5	4	23	3	14	2	51
Sexual offences	2	0	5	0	0	0	7
Burglary	52	2	57	6	52	1	170
Robbery	14	2	4	0	2	0	22
Theft	87	8	149	21	79	1	345
Fraud and forgery	2	0	11	1	7	0	21
Criminal damage	38	3	31	4	39	1	116
Offences against the state	2	4	1	0	2	0	9
Other offences	5	1	8	0	0	0	14
TOTAL INDICTABLE OFFENCES	207	24	289	35	195	5	755
SUMMARY [1]	12	3	49	20	67	29	180
MOTORING [2]	9	2	17	17	28	1	74
ALL OFFENCES	228	29	355	72	290	35	1009

TABLE 5.10: Percentage Juvenile disposals for each crime category at Magistrates' Courts and the Crown Court 1995

CRIME CATEGORY	Immediate Custody	Suspended Custody	Supervision in the Community	Fine	Conditional Discharge	Other	TOTAL
Violence against the person	10	8	45	6	27	4	100
Sexual offences	29	0	71	0	0	0	100
Burglary	31	1	34	4	31	1	100
Robbery	64	9	18	0	9	0	100
Theft	25	2	43	6	23	0	100
Fraud and forgery	10	0	52	5	33	0	100
Criminal damage	33	3	27	3	34	1	100
Offences against the state	22	44	11	0	22	0	100
Other offences	36	7	57	0	0	0	100
TOTAL INDICTABLE OFFENCES	27	3	38	5	26	1	100
SUMMARY [1]	7	2	27	11	37	16	100
MOTORING [2]	12	3	23	23	38	1	100
ALL OFFENCES	23	3	35	7	29	3	100

Note: (1)   Excluding Motoring Offences.
        (2)   Indictable and Summary Motoring Offences.
        (3)   Percentage components may not sum to 100% due to rounding.

TABLE 5.11: Juveniles: All Court Sentencing: Indictable and Summary offences 1986-1995

SENTENCE   NUMBER OF PERSONS

	1986	1987	1988	1989	1990	1991	1992	1993	1994	1995
Prison	3	2	2	3	2	0	1	0	0	0
Young Offenders' Centre	40	37	54	44	20	31	30	22	29	54
Training School	267	220	167	170	146	170	123	116	174	165
Total Immediate Custody	310	259	223	217	168	201	154	138	203	219
Prison Suspended/Recorded	4	6	5	4	0	1	0	1	0	2
YOC Suspended/Recorded	20	36	22	38	25	19	11	14	17	25
Attendance Centre	97	101	134	99	102	80	61	83	80	92
Probation/Supervision	304	215	248	209	220	172	168	163	183	219
Community Service Order	1	0	1	7	32	26	22	19	23	27
Fine	253	219	166	134	115	67	62	33	49	55
Recognizance	18	21	20	10	8	12	10	26	23	29
Conditional Discharge	423	354	255	206	198	211	199	244	218	262
Absolute Discharge	26	19	14	10	9	8	9	4	9	5
Fine plus Disqualification	7	9	6	3	5	2	2	0	0	0
Other	7	6	8	1	4	5	4	0	0	0
All Sentences	1470	1245	1102	938	886	804	702	725	805	935

PERCENTAGE OF ALL SENTENCES

	1986	1987	1988	1989	1990	1991	1992	1993	1994	1995
Prison	0	0	0	0	0	0	0	0	0	0
Young Offenders' Centre	3	3	5	5	2	4	4	3	4	6
Training School	18	18	15	18	16	21	18	16	21	18
Total Immediate Custody	21	21	20	23	19	25	22	19	25	23
Prison Suspended/Recorded	0	0	0	0	0	0	0	0	0	0
YOC Suspended/Recorded	1	3	2	4	3	2	2	2	2	3
Attendance Centre	7	8	12	11	12	10	9	11	10	10
Probation/Supervision	21	17	23	22	25	21	24	22	23	23
Community Service Order	0	0	0	1	4	3	3	3	3	3
Fine	17	18	15	14	13	8	9	5	6	6
Recognizance	1	2	2	1	1	1	1	4	3	3
Conditional Discharge	29	28	23	22	22	26	28	34	27	28
Absolute Discharge	2	2	1	1	1	1	1	1	1	1
Fine plus Disqualification	0	1	1	0	1	0	0	0	0	0
Other	0	0	1	0	0	1	1	0	0	0

Note: (1)   Excluding Motoring Offences.
        (2)   Percentage components may not sum to 100% due to rounding.

6. Prison population

6.1 Offenders given an immediate custodial sentence by the Court may be specifically directed to a Training School (if under 17), a Young Offenders Centre (if under 21 and receiving a sentence of up to 4 years) or may be given a more general order of imprisonment or detention. Training Schools are not prison service establishments and persons detained there are not included in this chapter. Some information on the use of Training Schools is included in Chapter 5 and Appendix 3. This chapter therefore provides information on the population of the establishments operated by the Northern Ireland Prison Service to hold persons in legal custody as directed by the courts.

6.2 The prison population consists mainly of offenders sentenced by the courts to immediate custody for criminal offences. It also includes fine defaulters, remand prisoners and a small number of non-criminal or civil prisoners. Immediate custody prisoners and fine defaulters are collectively referred to as sentenced prisoners.

6.3 Fine defaulters are those who have been given a fine by the courts (strictly a fine or custodial sentence), have not paid the fine within a stipulated time, and have then been the subject of a warrant issued by the court. They are a particular type of sentenced criminal prisoner. The duration of sentence is dependent upon the amount of the unpaid fine. This ranges in Magistrates' Courts from one week where the default is £200 or less, up to ten years where it is over £1 million. In the Crown Court the duration of sentence may not exceed 12 months for any amount. Fine defaulters aged under 17 are detained in a Training School, and are therefore excluded from the statistics in this chapter.

6.4 Remand prisoners include those charged with an offence whom the courts have ruled should be detained in custody pending trial; those whom the courts have permitted to be released on bail pending trial but have not as yet met the conditions (usually financial) of the bail; those who had been released on bail but have subsequently been re-admitted to prison because they breached a condition of bail; and those who have been found guilty by the court but have been ordered to be detained in custody pending sentence. Persons aged under 17 on remand will normally be detained in a Training School, and therefore may be excluded from the statistics in this chapter.

6.5 Non-criminal prisoners include those who have been imprisoned for non-payment of maintenance, non-payment of a debt, contempt of court, or are being held under the terms of an Immigration Act.

6.6 The prison population fluctuates throughout the year and within each week. This is as a consequence of factors such as the pattern of court sitting and discharge rules relating to weekends. To remove within-week variation and provide a more consistent approach, prison population statistics are based on counts taken on the last Thursday night of each month. *Annual averages* are derived from twelve such monthly counts. *Annual prison receptions* are calculated simply as the sum total of admissions into prisons during the year.

6.7 In general the counting rules in operation closely follow those used by the Home office. Important features of these are:-

- where a person is received more than once a year he will be counted separately on each occasion, including each occasion of change of status between remand and sentenced/fine defaulter;

- where a person is received under sentence for two or more offences, only the principal criminal offence is recorded;

- where a person is received under sentence for two or more offences, sentence length is taken as the longest of any concurrent sentences, with consecutive sentences being treated as one sentence equal in length to the sentences added together; and

- the age of a prisoner is calculated as age at reception.

The Average Daily
Prison Population

6.8 The *average prison population* in Northern Ireland declined steadily from a peak level in 1978 until 1990. Thereafter it had shown an upward trend (Figure 6.1) which was reversed again in 1994. In 1995 the average prison population fell by 7% to 1,762.

Figure 6.1: AVERAGE PRISON POPULATION 1969-1995

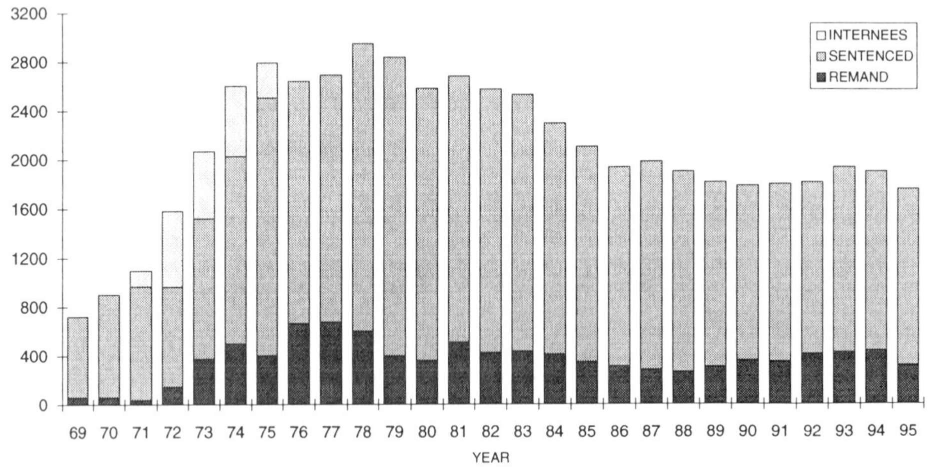

6.9 The decrease in average daily population is attributable to a fall in both the male population (1,727) and the average female population (35). The main decrease has been in the number on remand (males down 27% on 1994 and females down 58% on 1994). Remand prisoners now comprise 18% of the total prison population compared to 23% in 1994 (Figure 6.2).

Figure 6.2: AVERAGE PRISON POPULATION BY AGE AND SEX 1986-1995

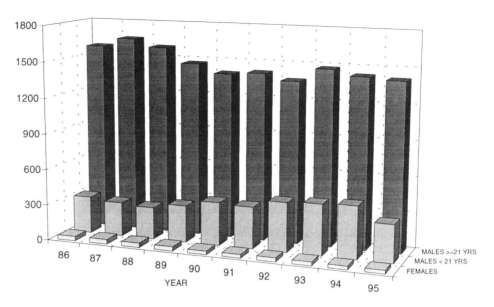

Offenders sentenced to immediate custody

6.10 The average number of persons in prison in 1995 who had been sentenced to immediate custody was 1,411, down 1% on the previous year. Of the 1,411 immediate custody population in 1995, 1,198 were adults aged 21 and over, and 213 were aged under 21 on reception (Table 6.1).

6.11 The age profile of the average prison population is markedly different from the overall Northern Ireland population. In 1995 64% of the average prison population who had been sentenced to immediate custody were between the ages of 17 and 29, with 49% being between the ages of 21 and 29 (Figure 6.3). The equivalent proportions for the population as a whole are 20% (17-29) and 14% (21-29). Over the years there has been a general downward trend in the prison population of the average number of prisoners aged under 21 when they were sentenced to immediate custody. Following a drop in 1994 compared to 1993, the average fell again in 1995 by 8% on the previous year (Table 6.3).

Figure 6.3: AVERAGE PRISON POPULATION UNDER SENTENCE OF IMMEDIATE CUSTODY - BY AGE - 1995

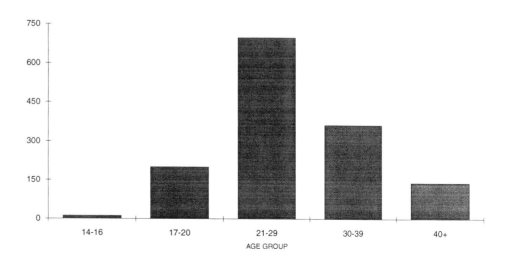

6.12 On average in 1995, 56% of those in prison sentenced to immediate custody had committed offences of violence against the person, 13% offences of dishonesty (theft, fraud & forgery, and burglary), 11% offences of robbery, 7% sexual offences, 3% drug offences, and 2% criminal damage offences (Table 6.4). The average number of sexual offenders in the prison population (101 in 1995) is the lowest since 1989. It is however 42% higher than the 1986 average (Figure 6.4). Sexual offenders in 1995 account for 8% of the average daily sentenced population (excluding fine defaulters) compared to 4% in 1985.

Figure 6.4: AVERAGE PRISON POPULATION UNDER SENTENCE OF IMMEDIATE CUSTODY 1986-1995

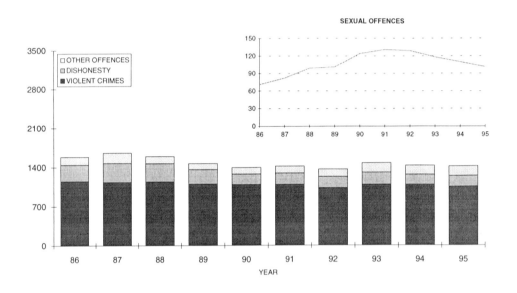

Prison Receptions

6.13 Receptions into prison have been rising annually by about 3-4% from 1990 to 1993. In 1995 receptions in prison rose again to 5,088, a 4% increase on 1994 (4,897). The increase is a combination of a 31% drop in female remand prisoners from 102 in 1994 to a 1995 figure of 70; an 11% increase in male fine defaulters from 1,408 in 1994 to 1,559 in 1995 and an overall increase in immediate custody receptions of 5% to 1,441 in 1995. Receptions of male non-criminal prisoners rose by almost 250% from 13 in 1994 to 45 in 1995.

6.14 The number of fine defaulters received into prison in 1995 was 1,599. While this represents an increase of 9% on the previous year, fine defaulters as a percentage of total receptions remained at 30-31% in 1995, the same proportion as in 1994.

Figure 6.5: PRISON RECEPTIONS 1986-1995

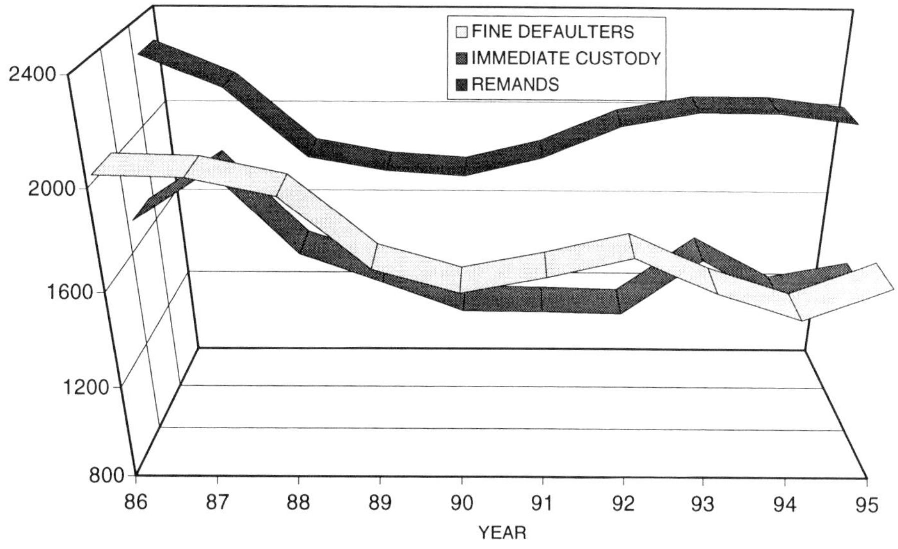

FINE DEFAULTERS
IMMEDIATE CUSTODY
REMANDS
2400
2000
1600
1200
800
86
87
88
89
90
91
92
93
94
95
YEAR

Comparisons between Receptions and the Daily Population

6.15 Short sentence prisoners account for the greater proportion of receptions into prison. However given their turnover most of the sentenced prison population at any time are in custody for lengthy sentences. On average in 1995, 14% of those in prison who had been sentenced to immediate custody, had sentences of up to 1 year, 26% had sentences of between 1 and 5 years, 42% had determinate sentences of over 5 years, and 18% were serving life sentences (including those detained at the Secretary of State's pleasure). By contrast, receptions into prison show a different pattern. In 1995, 63% of those sentenced to immediate custody were given sentences of 1 year or less, 26% received sentences between 1 and 5 years, 9% had determinate sentences of over 5 years, and only 2% received life sentences (Figures 6.6 and 6.7).

Figure 6.6: AVERAGE PRISON POPULATION UNDER SENTENCE OF IMMEDIATE CUSTODY 1995

< 1 yr
14%
Life
18%
1-5 yrs
26%
> 5 yrs
42%

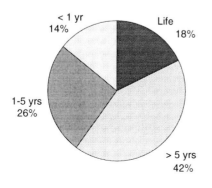

Figure 6.7: RECEPTIONS UNDER SENTENCE OF IMMEDIATE CUSTODY 1995

Life
2%
> 5yrs
9%
1-5 yrs
26%
< 1 yr
63%

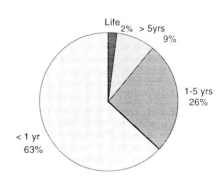

Percentages may not sum to 100% due to rounding.

6.16 Despite constituting a small part of the prison population (daily average 29 or 2% of total in 1995) a substantial number of persons are admitted to prison each year because of fine default. The number of annual receptions rose by 9% in 1995 to 1,599. This number is the highest number of receptions for fine default in the last 3 years and continues a trend where more persons are still received into prison for fine default than those received under sentence of immediate custody - this has held true for each of the last ten years.

6.17 The average remand population in 1995 decreased by 122 to 317, a drop of 28% on 1994. The reception of remand prisoners fell by 2% from 2,043 in 1994 to 2,003 in 1995.

6.18 Non-criminal prisoners comprise only a small part of both the average prison population and prison receptions. However, there was an average of 5 non-criminal prisoners during 1995, a substantial proportionate increase on the average of only one non-criminal prisoner from 1990 to 1994. As regards receptions of these prisoners, the number rose sharply from 13 in 1994 to 45 in 1995.

TABLE 6.1: Average population in prison establishments, by type of prisoner 1986-1995

	1986	1987	1988	1989	1990	1991	1992	1993	1994	1995
Male Prisoners										
Remand										
Aged Under 21	117	84	70	82	87	79	93	96	106	72
Aged 21 or Over	187	194	188	217	259	254	307	322	321	240
	304	278	258	299	346	333	400	418	427	312
Fine defaulter										
Aged Under 21	9	11	8	7	6	8	6	7	4	5
Aged 21 or Over	27	27	29	28	23	23	27	23	23	23
	36	38	37	35	29	31	33	30	27	28
Immediate Custody										
YOC	186	219	170	156	134	141	145	153	133	118
Young Prisoners	261	244	210	165	140	116	102	100	91	87
Adult Prisoners	1112	1168	1193	1129	1105	1136	1088	1192	1179	1177
	1559	1631	1573	1450	1379	1393	1335	1445	1403	1382
Non-Criminal	7	3	4	6	1	1	1	1	1	5
All Males	1906	1950	1872	1790	1755	1758	1769	1894	1858	1727
Female Prisoners										
Remand										
Aged Under 21	2	1	1	2	6	6	6	2	5	2
Aged 21 or Over	4	5	7	6	8	10	7	6	7	3
	6	6	8	8	14	16	13	8	12	5
Fine defaulter										
Aged Under 21	0	0	0	0	0	0	0	1	1	0
Aged 21 or Over	1	1	1	1	1	1	1	1	2	1
	1	1	1	1	1	1	1	2	3	1
Immediate Custody										
YOC	2	2	1	3	2	2	4	3	4	6
Young Prisoners	2	2	2	1	1	1	2	3	3	2
Adult Prisoners	20	20	17	12	12	18	21	24	19	21
	24	24	20	16	15	21	27	30	26	29
Non-Criminal	0	0	0	0	0	0	0	0	0	0
All Females	31	31	29	25	30	38	41	40	41	35
All Prisoners										
Remand	310	284	266	307	360	349	413	426	439	317
Fine Defaulter	37	39	38	36	30	32	34	32	30	29
Immediate Custody	1583	1655	1593	1466	1394	1414	1362	1475	1429	1411
Non-Criminal	7	3	4	6	1	1	1	1	1	5
TOTAL	1937	1981	1901	1815	1785	1796	1810	1934	1899	1762

TABLE 6.2: Average prison population under sentence of immediate custody, by duration of sentence given 1986-1995

	1986	1987	1988	1989	1990	1991	1992	1993	1994	1995
Adult Males										
Life	335	336	340	337	315	309	270	262	225	232
>10 years, less than life	188	160	169	169	184	209	207	252	282	278
>5 and <=10 years	156	145	177	204	226	242	220	226	244	241
>4 and <=5 years	52	71	83	73	68	67	70	83	88	76
>3 and <=4 years	62	83	80	69	57	58	61	73	62	65
>2 and <=3 years	78	96	100	68	61	57	67	76	67	72
>1 and <=2 years	88	104	94	75	74	77	70	83	86	87
>6 and <=12 months	79	97	84	69	67	60	68	79	72	66
>3 and <=6 months	60	59	53	51	43	46	41	46	40	50
<=3 months	17	18	15	13	10	12	16	12	12	10
TOTAL	1112	1168	1193	1129	1105	1136	1088	1192	1179	1177
Young Males										
Life	122	106	98	86	62	45	35	26	18	17
>10 years, less than life	73	52	36	27	29	26	23	27	29	27
>5 and <=10 years	36	42	40	35	36	35	37	41	37	35
>4 and <=5 years	15	22	24	17	13	9	7	7	7	7
>3 and <=4 years	15	22	13	9	18	23	28	29	23	19
>2 and <=3 years	53	68	57	35	28	36	29	23	26	16
>1 and <=2 years	46	61	39	41	31	30	31	38	28	23
>6 and <=12 months	44	49	43	38	32	28	25	35	36	33
>3 and <=6 months	35	34	26	26	19	21	26	24	18	22
<=3 months	9	7	6	6	6	3	5	5	3	5
TOTAL	447	463	380	321	274	257	247	253	224	205
Adult Females										
Life	5	6	6	6	6	4	3	4	5	6
>5 years, less than life	9	6	3	1	2	5	7	9	8	9
>1 and <=5 years	3	3	5	1	3	7	10	8	3	2
>6 and <=12 months	2	3	1	2	1	0	1	3	0	4
>3 and <=6 months	1	2	1	2	1	1	1	1	2	1
<=3 months	1	1	1	1	0	1	0	1	1	1
TOTAL	20	20	17	12	13	18	21	24	19	21
Young Females										
Life	0	0	0	0	0	0	0	0	0	0
>5 years, less than life	2	2	1	1	1	1	2	3	3	2
>1 and <=5 years	0	0	1	2	1	1	3	2	1	3
>6 and <=12 months	0	1	0	0	0	1	1	0	1	2
>3 and <=6 months	1	0	0	0	0	0	0	1	1	1
<=3 months	0	1	0	0	0	0	0	0	1	0
TOTAL	4	4	3	4	2	3	6	6	7	8

Notes: (1) Components may not sum to totals due to rounding.
(2) Life includes those detained at the Secretary of State's Pleasure.

TABLE 6.3: Average prison population under sentence of immediate custody, by age at reception 1986-1995

	1986	1987	1988	1989	1990	1991	1992	1993	1994	1995
Male										
14 - 16 years	14	17	14	12	12	8	11	13	8	12
17 - 20 years	433	446	367	308	262	248	234	239	215	193
21 - 29 years	797	840	832	760	722	713	669	719	707	686
30 - 39 years	235	242	260	266	278	301	298	331	341	357
40 - 49 years	67	72	79	81	77	90	90	97	87	91
50 - 59 years	10	10	17	14	19	24	26	34	34	31
60 + years	3	4	6	8	8	9	5	10	11	11
TOTAL	1559	1631	1573	1450	1379	1393	1335	1445	1403	1382
Female										
14 - 16 years	0	1	0	0	1	0	1	1	1	1
17 - 20 years	4	4	2	3	2	3	5	5	5	7
21 - 29 years	14	15	12	9	8	10	15	13	9	11
30 - 39 years	2	1	2	1	2	6	5	8	6	5
40 - 49 years	3	3	3	2	3	2	2	3	3	5
50 - 59 years	0	1	1	1	0	0	0	0	0	0
60 + years	0	0	0	0	0	0	0	0	0	0
TOTAL	24	24	20	16	15	21	27	30	26	29
Male and Female										
14 - 16 years	14	18	14	12	13	9	12	14	10	12
17 - 20 years	437	450	369	311	264	251	239	244	220	200
21 - 29 years	811	855	844	769	730	722	684	732	717	697
30 - 39 years	237	243	262	267	280	307	303	339	347	362
40 - 49 years	70	75	82	83	80	92	91	100	90	97
50 - 59 years	10	11	18	15	19	24	26	34	34	31
60 + years	3	4	6	8	8	9	5	10	11	11
TOTAL	1583	1655	1593	1466	1394	1414	1362	1475	1429	1411

Notes: (1)   Components may not sum to totals due to rounding.

TABLE 6.4: Average prison population under sentence of immediate custody, by offence 1986-1995

	1986	1987	1988	1989	1990	1991	1992	1993	1994	1995
Adult Male										
Violence against the person	645	624	638	628	621	642	596	666	690	694
Sexual offences	63	67	82	89	103	107	110	102	96	92
Burglary	118	128	120	88	69	58	64	74	62	65
Robbery	123	138	161	166	170	151	141	151	146	126
Theft	57	74	81	63	41	57	54	57	50	48
Fraud & forgery	22	27	29	24	28	33	25	33	23	25
Criminal damage	38	50	32	20	18	24	24	27	19	19
Drugs offences	2	4	8	9	5	4	6	11	26	37
Motoring offences	38	41	36	20	29	23	23	28	28	30
Other offences	36	43	39	22	22	38	45	44	40	42
TOTAL	1112	1168	1193	1129	1105	1136	1088	1192	1180	1177
Young Male										
Violence against the person	258	232	198	165	135	121	105	95	84	82
Sexual offences	8	15	16	12	21	24	19	16	14	9
Burglary	64	73	65	50	32	33	34	33	29	32
Robbery	38	41	32	33	30	28	41	37	40	31
Theft	23	25	23	23	14	19	16	12	11	12
Fraud & forgery	2	4	3	3	1	2	1	2	1	0
Criminal damage	31	49	27	17	22	15	12	23	13	9
Drugs offences	1	0	0	1	0	0	0	6	5	6
Motoring offences	13	18	15	12	13	9	15	22	20	18
Other offences	23	19	10	5	6	5	4	7	7	7
TOTAL	447	463	380	321	274	257	247	253	224	205
Adult Female										
Violence against the person	14	14	13	8	9	13	16	18	14	14
Sexual offences	0	0	1	0	0	0	0	0	0	0
Burglary	0	0	0	0	0	0	0	0	0	0
Robbery	0	0	0	0	1	1	0	1	1	2
Theft	4	4	2	3	1	1	2	2	1	4
Fraud & forgery	1	2	1	1	1	2	1	1	1	1
Criminal damage	1	1	0	0	0	0	1	0	0	1
Drugs offences	0	0	0	0	0	0	0	2	1	0
Motoring offences	0	0	0	0	0	0	0	0	0	1
Other offences	0	1	1	0	1	2	1	0	0	0
TOTAL	20	20	17	12	13	18	21	24	19	21
Young Female										
Violence against the person	2	2	2	3	1	2	4	6	3	3
Sexual offences	0	0	0	0	0	0	0	0	0	0
Burglary	0	0	0	0	0	0	0	0	0	0
Robbery	0	0	0	0	0	1	1	0	0	1
Theft	1	1	1	0	0	0	1	0	1	1
Fraud & forgery	0	0	0	0	0	0	0	0	0	1
Criminal damage	1	0	0	0	0	0	0	0	0	0
Drugs offences	0	0	0	0	0	0	0	0	0	0
Motoring offences	0	0	0	0	0	0	0	0	0	0
Other offences	0	1	1	0	1	0	1	0	1	2
TOTAL	4	4	3	4	2	3	6	6	7	8

Notes: (1) Components may not sum to totals due to rounding.

TABLE 6.5: Average prison population under sentence of immediate custody, scheduled and non-scheduled offences 1986-1995

	1986	1987	1988	1989	1990	1991	1992	1993	1994	1995
Scheduled Offences										
Adult Male	820	826	848	832	829	849	802	883	887	872
Young Male	331	336	264	223	193	172	161	159	142	124
Adult Female	14	15	14	8	11	15	18	19	15	15
Young Female	3	2	2	3	2	2	5	5	4	5
TOTAL	1168	1179	1128	1066	1035	1038	986	1066	1048	1016
Non-Scheduled Offences										
Adult Male	322	370	378	297	276	287	287	309	293	305
Young Male	129	139	126	98	81	85	86	94	81	81
Adult Female	6	7	4	4	2	3	3	5	4	6
Young Female	1	2	2	0	0	1	1	0	3	3
TOTAL	458	518	510	399	359	376	377	408	381	395
TOTAL	1626	1697	1638	1466	1394	1414	1363	1475	1429	1411

Notes: (1) Components may not sum to totals due to rounding.
(2) From 1989 the scheduled/non-scheduled categories include only persons sentenced to immediate custody by the courts; figures prior to 1989 included others, such as fine defaulters and non-criminal prisoners.

TABLE 6.6: Receptions into prison establishments, by type of prisoner 1986-1995

	1986	1987	1988	1989	1990	1991	1992	1993	1994	1995
Male Prisoners										
Remand										
Aged Under 21	925	756	589	623	528	500	596	641	579	627
Aged 21 or Over	1270	1303	1182	1085	1165	1257	1301	1333	1362	1306
	2195	2059	1771	1708	1693	1757	1897	1974	1941	1933
Fine defaulter										
Aged Under 21	545	507	447	371	296	344	357	335	267	343
Aged 21 or Over	1413	1436	1441	1248	1226	1248	1314	1188	1141	1216
	1958	1943	1888	1619	1522	1592	1671	1523	1408	1559
Immediate Custody										
YOC	576	565	430	415	365	339	363	407	332	356
Young Prisoners	55	44	25	30	24	18	15	23	14	14
Adult Prisoners	1040	1268	1085	974	914	932	903	1086	991	1022
	1671	1877	1540	1419	1303	1289	1281	1516	1337	1392
Non-Criminal	16	22	50	46	21	17	10	20	13	45
All Males	5840	5901	5249	4792	4539	4655	4859	5033	4699	4929
Female Prisoners										
Remand										
Aged Under 21	33	24	18	30	30	28	28	21	47	23
Aged 21 or Over	45	57	64	57	50	66	62	50	55	47
	78	81	82	87	80	94	90	71	102	70
Fine defaulter										
Aged Under 21	21	21	10	7	13	12	7	18	9	8
Aged 21 or Over	49	56	52	43	38	34	38	33	49	32
	70	77	62	50	51	46	45	51	58	40
Immediate Custody										
YOC	11	11	7	7	6	9	8	9	14	15
Young Prisoners	0	1	1	0	0	2	0	1	0	0
Adult Prisoners	31	30	25	25	15	22	23	25	24	34
	42	42	33	32	21	33	31	35	38	49
Non-Criminal	0	1	0	0	0	0	0	1	0	0
All Females	190	201	177	169	152	173	166	158	198	159
All Prisoners										
Remand	2273	2140	1853	1795	1773	1851	1987	2045	2043	2003
Fine Defaulter	2028	2020	1950	1669	1573	1638	1716	1574	1466	1599
Immediate Custody	1713	1919	1573	1451	1324	1322	1312	1551	1375	1441
Non-Criminal	16	23	50	46	21	17	10	21	13	45
TOTAL	6030	6102	5426	4961	4691	4828	5025	5191	4897	5088

Notes: (1) Figures shown for the YOC relate to sentences to the YOC establishment. For administrative reasons, the male figures may not equate precisely with the number of persons placed in YOC Hydebank.

TABLE 6.7: Receptions under sentence of immediate custody, by duration of sentence given 1986-1995

	1986	1987	1988	1989	1990	1991	1992	1993	1994	1995
Adult Males										
Life	23	14	14	16	16	16	16	19	23	23
>10 years, less than life	24	39	37	32	40	45	32	78	32	51
>5 and <=10 years	53	60	83	74	74	84	55	74	75	68
>4 and <=5 years	30	44	35	37	33	40	33	40	35	32
>3 and <=4 years	50	55	36	35	29	37	33	52	43	53
>2 and <=3 years	77	90	59	56	47	56	63	69	50	83
>1 and <=2 years	129	170	119	103	110	115	107	139	145	134
>6 and <=12 months	208	263	232	182	189	172	184	227	207	189
>3 and <=6 months	270	300	265	265	226	219	212	247	223	254
<=3 months	176	233	205	174	150	148	168	141	158	135
TOTAL	1040	1268	1085	974	914	932	903	1086	991	1022
Young Males										
Life	1	3	4	3	1	1	1	0	0	3
>10 years, less than life	4	5	1	5	3	5	1	10	3	2
>5 and <=10 years	21	14	11	12	16	9	10	8	7	7
>4 and <=5 years	10	16	5	10	4	3	3	5	4	2
>3 and <=4 years	19	6	4	11	12	17	11	22	14	12
>2 and <=3 years	66	57	36	20	28	29	17	25	21	15
>1 and <=2 years	86	87	54	56	44	45	47	51	44	43
>6 and <=12 months	140	145	119	108	97	94	79	112	102	98
>3 and <=6 months	179	186	145	137	114	104	134	139	103	124
<=3 months	105	90	76	83	70	50	75	58	48	64
TOTAL	631	609	455	445	389	357	378	430	346	370
Adult Females										
Life	4	0	0	0	0	0	0	1	2	0
>5 years, less than life	1	0	0	1	1	2	4	1	1	2
>1 and <=5 years	4	6	2	2	7	4	9	4	1	3
>6 and <=12 months	7	8	4	7	2	0	2	7	1	9
>3 and <=6 months	7	9	6	9	2	8	4	3	12	6
<=3 months	8	7	13	6	3	8	4	9	7	14
TOTAL	31	30	25	25	15	22	23	25	24	34
Young Females										
Life	0	0	0	0	0	0	0	0	0	0
>5 years, less than life	0	1	0	0	0	2	0	1	0	0
>1 and <=5 years	1	0	2	2	2	2	3	0	3	2
>6 and <=12 months	0	2	1	0	1	0	2	0	2	6
>3 and <=6 months	6	0	2	3	0	2	2	3	4	2
<=3 months	4	9	3	2	3	5	1	6	5	5
TOTAL	11	12	8	7	6	11	8	10	14	15

Notes: (1)   Life includes those detained at the Secretary of State's Pleasure.

TABLE 6.8: Receptions under sentence of immediate custody, by age at reception 1986-1995

	1986	1987	1988	1989	1990	1991	1992	1993	1994	1995
Male										
14 - 16 years	29	34	35	41	23	20	25	16	23	49
17 - 20 years	602	575	420	404	366	337	353	414	323	321
21 - 29 years	729	892	698	615	611	586	581	682	608	587
30 - 39 years	193	241	264	248	212	234	204	270	278	296
40 - 49 years	88	99	87	80	62	82	74	90	72	89
50 - 59 years	25	26	29	26	22	22	33	29	21	39
60 + years	5	10	7	5	7	8	11	15	12	11
TOTAL	1671	1877	1540	1419	1303	1289	1281	1516	1337	1392
Female										
14 - 16 years	0	3	3	0	1	1	1	0	3	0
17 - 20 years	11	9	5	7	5	10	7	10	11	15
21 - 29 years	21	18	11	15	11	12	20	14	12	14
30 - 39 years	6	6	10	4	2	5	2	7	9	13
40 - 49 years	3	5	4	2	2	4	1	4	3	6
50 - 59 years	1	1	0	4	0	1	0	0	0	1
60 + years	0	0	0	0	0	0	0	0	0	0
TOTAL	42	42	33	32	21	33	31	35	38	49
Male and Female										
14 - 16 years	29	37	38	41	24	21	26	16	26	49
17 - 20 years	613	584	425	411	371	347	360	424	334	336
21 - 29 years	750	910	709	630	622	598	601	696	620	601
30 - 39 years	199	247	274	252	214	239	206	277	287	309
40 - 49 years	91	104	91	82	64	86	75	94	75	95
50 - 59 years	26	27	29	30	22	23	33	29	21	40
60 + years	5	10	7	5	7	8	11	15	12	11
TOTAL	1713	1919	1573	1451	1324	1322	1312	1551	1375	1441

TABLE 6.9: Receptions under sentence of immediate custody, by offence 1986-1995

	1986	1987	1988	1989	1990	1991	1992	1993	1994	1995
Adult Male										
Violence against the person	232	264	217	205	219	228	188	344	266	263
Sexual offences	46	71	78	56	70	68	63	57	55	60
Burglary	223	218	191	155	145	120	106	144	117	120
Robbery	84	102	102	109	82	75	93	59	68	60
Theft	152	196	192	190	142	173	171	161	133	132
Fraud & forgery	44	57	46	46	35	44	36	48	35	54
Criminal damage	65	94	45	48	41	43	48	62	64	51
Drugs offences	4	12	8	7	5	7	8	30	56	81
Motoring offences	107	119	116	89	111	88	99	116	133	122
Other offences	83	135	90	69	64	86	91	65	64	79
TOTAL	1040	1268	1085	974	914	932	903	1086	991	1022
Young Male										
Violence against the person	126	101	78	78	83	74	55	76	50	44
Sexual offences	7	25	8	13	18	7	9	8	4	6
Burglary	153	168	127	121	80	73	83	81	67	94
Robbery	43	29	35	35	25	36	35	30	29	23
Theft	83	84	72	77	61	67	66	47	43	51
Fraud & forgery	8	7	8	8	10	5	2	5	5	1
Criminal damage	95	62	44	36	28	30	29	55	27	21
Drugs offences	2	0	1	0	0	0	2	14	10	21
Motoring offences	41	71	61	54	53	44	73	87	93	89
Other offences	73	62	21	23	31	21	24	27	18	20
TOTAL	631	609	455	445	389	357	378	430	346	370
Adult Female										
Violence against the person	8	4	3	2	4	4	10	7	9	3
Sexual offences	0	1	0	0	0	0	0	0	0	1
Burglary	0	0	0	1	0	0	1	0	2	1
Robbery	0	1	0	0	1	1	0	1	2	0
Theft	20	14	15	14	4	10	6	7	7	14
Fraud & forgery	1	4	3	6	2	3	1	3	1	6
Criminal damage	2	3	0	2	1	1	2	0	0	4
Drugs offences	0	0	0	0	0	0	0	3	0	0
Motoring offences	0	0	0	0	0	2	0	0	2	3
Other offences	0	3	4	0	3	1	3	4	1	2
TOTAL	31	30	25	25	15	22	23	25	24	34
Young Female										
Violence against the person	2	1	2	2	1	3	3	5	2	2
Sexual offences	0	0	0	0	0	0	0	0	0	1
Burglary	0	1	0	2	0	0	1	1	2	0
Robbery	1	0	0	0	1	1	0	0	0	2
Theft	3	5	2	3	2	4	2	3	4	4
Fraud & forgery	0	0	1	0	0	0	0	0	2	1
Criminal damage	3	0	1	0	1	0	0	0	1	0
Drugs offences	0	0	0	0	0	0	0	0	0	1
Motoring offences	0	0	0	0	0	1	1	1	0	0
Other offences	2	5	2	0	1	2	1	0	3	4
TOTAL	11	12	8	7	6	11	8	10	14	15

TABLE 6.10: Receptions under sentence of immediate custody, scheduled and non-scheduled offences 1986-1995

	1986	1987	1988	1989	1990	1991	1992	1993	1994	1995
Scheduled Offences										
Adult Male	386	447	347	349	320	362	342	466	386	379
Young Male	269	205	147	140	132	133	118	155	110	83
Adult Female	8	7	6	4	8	7	12	6	7	6
Young Female	4	1	2	3	4	4	3	3	3	5
TOTAL	667	660	502	496	464	506	475	630	506	473
Non-Scheduled Offences										
Adult Male	654	821	738	625	594	570	561	620	605	643
Young Male	362	404	308	305	257	224	260	275	236	287
Adult Female	23	23	19	21	7	15	11	19	17	28
Young Female	7	11	6	4	2	7	5	7	11	10
TOTAL	1046	1259	1071	955	860	816	837	921	869	968
TOTAL	1713	1919	1573	1451	1324	1322	1312	1551	1375	1441

TABLE 6.11: Discharges from prison establishments, by type of prisoner 1986-1995

	1986	1987	1988	1989	1990	1991	1992	1993	1994	1995
Male Prisoners										
Remand										
Aged Under 21	942	756	613	558	510	498	581	631	580	656
Aged 21 or Over	1263	1276	1190	959	1097	1229	1272	1335	1301	1450
	2205	2032	1803	1517	1607	1727	1853	1966	1881	2106
Fine defaulter										
Aged Under 21	546	511	446	337	295	341	356	337	269	341
Aged 21 or Over	1401	1442	1441	1118	1225	1252	1314	1191	1139	1219
	1947	1953	1887	1455	1520	1593	1670	1528	1408	1560
Immediate Custody										
YOC	563	560	493	402	369	343	390	407	351	360
Young Prisoners	92	52	71	54	48	34	26	28	25	29
Adult Prisoners	1110	1145	1141	970	938	949	937	1038	1040	1096
	1765	1757	1705	1426	1355	1326	1353	1473	1416	1485
Non-Criminal	17	28	42	57	23	16	10	21	13	36
All Males	5934	5770	5437	4455	4505	4662	4886	4988	4718	5187
Female Prisoners										
Remand										
Aged Under 21	33	24	20	25	21	27	32	19	47	27
Aged 21 or Over	47	57	62	71	44	62	67	51	58	49
	80	81	82	96	65	89	99	70	105	76
Fine defaulter										
Aged Under 21	21	21	10	7	14	12	7	18	9	8
Aged 21 or Over	49	56	52	40	39	34	38	33	49	32
	70	77	62	47	53	46	45	51	58	40
Immediate Custody										
YOC	13	11	7	7	7	9	4	12	12	15
Young Prisoners	2	0	1	0	1	0	0	0	0	2
Adult Prisoners	29	33	31	23	13	24	15	28	25	35
	44	44	39	30	21	33	19	40	37	52
Non-Criminal	0	1	0	0	0	0	0	1	0	0
All Females	194	203	183	173	139	168	163	162	200	168
All Prisoners										
Remand	2285	2113	1885	1613	1672	1816	1952	2036	1986	2182
Fine Defaulter	2017	2030	1949	1502	1573	1639	1715	1579	1466	1600
Immediate Custody	1809	1801	1744	1456	1376	1359	1372	1513	1453	1537
Non-Criminal	17	29	42	57	23	16	10	22	13	36
TOTAL	6128	5973	5620	4628	4644	4830	5049	5150	4918	5355

Notes: (1) Figures shown for the YOC relate to sentences to the YOC establishment. For administrative reasons, the male figures may not equate precisely with the number of persons placed in YOC Hydebank.

Coverage of notifiable and indictable offences

1. In England and Wales classification of offences recorded by the police is based on a list of 'notifiable offences' which the Home Office requires to be notified by the various police forces. A separate, similar, but slightly different list of 'indictable offences' is issued for classifying the more serious offences which are the subject of court proceedings (Indictable offences are essentially those for which proceedings can or must be heard in the Crown Court - see Appendix 2).

2. In Northern Ireland the classification systems used for both offences recorded by the police and court proceedings are broadly similar to those in use in England and Wales. The same terminology is used, though some differences do occur, largely because of differences in legislation. Column 1 of the table overleaf comprises a list of offences grouped under 11 main headings. By reference to this list columns 2 and 3 indicate the approximate coverage of notifiable and indictable offences for England and Wales, and for Northern Ireland. Generally, attempting, conspiring, inciting, abetting, causing or permitting a crime is included with the crime itself, though in some cases it is shown separately.

3. The terms 'theft', 'burglary', and 'robbery' are often confused. They can be thought of as follows:

(a) Theft: The dishonest appropriation of another's property with the intention of permanently depriving the owner of it.

(b) Burglary: Entering a building as a trespasser with the intention of committing theft, rape, grievous bodily harm or unlawful damage. If a person commits the above offence whilst in possession of a weapon, or explosive the offence becomes aggravated burglary for which the maximum penalty is imprisonment for life.

(c) Robbery: The use or threat of force to a person immediately before or at the time of theft.

OFFENCE CATEGORY	NOTIFIABLE OFFENCES	INDICTABLE OFFENCES
I **Violence against the person**		
Murder	The following are excluded in both	All are included in both E&W and N.I.
Attempted murder	E&W and N.I.	A specific offence of intimidation is
Threat or conspiracy to murder	-Manslaughter due to diminished	included in N.I.
Manslaughter	responsibility.	
Infanticide	-Cruelty to or neglect of children.	
Child destruction	-Some acts endangering life at sea.	
Causing death by reckless driving		
Manslaughter due to diminished		
responsibility		
Wounding or other act	A specific offence of intimidation is	
endangering life	included in N.I.	
Endangering railway passenger		
Endangering life at sea		
Other wounding etc.		
Assault		
Cruelty to or neglect of children		
Abandoning child under two		
years		
Child abduction		
Procuring illegal abortion		
Concealment of birth		
II **Sexual offences**	Soliciting by a man is excluded in	All included in both E&W and N.I.
	both E&W and N.I.	
III **Burglary**	Going equipped for stealing is	All included in both E&W and N.I.
	counted in the 'other indictable'	
	category in E&W, but as burglary in	
	N.I.	
IV **Robbery**	In N.I. includes the specific offence	In N.I. includes the specific offence of
	of 'hijacking'.	'hijacking'.
V **Theft and handling stolen goods**	All included in both E&W and N.I.	All included in both E&W and N.I.

VI	**Fraud & forgery**	Offences relating to bankruptcy are all excluded in E&W but only some in N.I.	Copyright offences are included in N.I. In E&W they are classified as 'other indictable'.
VII	**Criminal Damage**	In England and Wales all criminal damage offences are in theory covered. In N.I. coverage is restricted to offences where damage exceeds £200.	Offences where damage is less than £400 are summary in nature, but are included in N.I.
VIII	**Other indictable offences (non-motoring)** **Drug offences** **Blackmail** **Kidnapping**	Includes 'going equipped for stealing' in E&W. Most offences from 'betting, gaming and lotteries' onwards are excluded in both E&W and N.I. Some minor differences in coverage occur. 'Treason', 'riot', 'unlawful assembly' and 'other offences against the state' are presented as a separate category in N.I. Some summary offences are included (see below).	Some differences in coverage arise between E&W and N.I. because of legislative differences. 'Treason', 'riot', 'unlawful assembly' and 'other offences against the state' are presented as a separate category in N.I.
IX	**Indictable motoring offences** **Reckless driving offences** **Driving licence offences** **Operator's licence** **Vehicle insurance offences** **Vehicle registration and licensing offences** **Driver's work record and employment offences** **Vehicle testing offences**	Excluded in both E&W and N.I.	Only a single category of motoring offences (indictable and summary) is identified in N.I.

X	Summary offences (non-motoring)	Almost all are excluded in both E&W and N.I. summary criminal damage cases in E&W and N.I. are included with indictable offences.	In E&W and N.I. summary criminal damage offences are included with indictable offences. A small number of 'other' offences are also included as indictable in both E&W and N.I.
	Aggravated assault		
	Assault on a constable		
	Brothel keeping		
	Cruelty to a child		
	Interference with motor vehicle	A few other offences are included under the heading 'Other notifiable offences'.	Some difference in coverage occurs between E&W and N.I. because of legislative differences.
	Indecent exposure		
	Summary offences of criminal or malicious damage		
	Unlawful possession		
	Found in enclosed premises		
	Summary drug offences		
	Summary immigration offences		
	Impersonating a police officer		
XI	**Summary offences (Motoring)**	Miscellaneous summary motoring offences.	All excluded in both E&W and N.I.
	Unfit to drive through drink or drugs		
	Racing reckless driving		Only a single category of motoring offences (indictable and summary) is identified in N.I. at present.
	Speeding - road limits		
	Speeding - vehicle limits		
	Motorway offences (excluding speeding)		
	Careless driving		
	Playstreet offences		
	Prohibited driving		
	Neglect of traffic directions		
	Obstruction (waiting and parking place offences)		
	Lighting offences		
	Vehicle or part in dangerous condition. Vehicle or part in defective condition. Trailer offences		
	Motor Cycle offences		
	Load offences		

Noise offences

Driving licence offences

Vehicle insurance offences

Vehicle registration and licensing (Excise) offences

Work record and employment offences

Accident offences

Vehicle testing offences and proscribed goods vehicle testing and planting offences

The criminal courts in Northern Ireland

1. Some crimes are obviously less serious than others. Less serious criminal offences are dealt with by way of summary trial in a Magistrates' Court (sometimes referred to as a Court of petty sessions). These offences include assaults, minor offences of dishonesty, (theft, handling stolen goods and deception) and offences against the Road Traffic (Northern Ireland) Order 1981. The trial takes place before a Resident Magistrate sitting alone, there is no jury, the Magistrate decides issues of law and fact, and on conviction passes sentence.

2. The more serious crimes like murder, robbery and rape are tried on indictment in the Crown Court by a judge and jury; though initially committal proceedings will also have been heard in the Magistrates' Court, where the Magistrate decides if there is sufficient evidence to merit the accused being sent for trial. In the Crown Court the judge decides all issues of law but questions of fact are left to be resolved by the jury who will decide whether or not the accused is guilty of the offence with which he is charged. The judge of course will pass sentence if the accused is convicted.

3. Paragraphs 1 and 2 outline the two main forms of procedure and trial. In Northern Ireland, however, since 1973 a special procedure has developed for dealing with serious offences relating to terrorism, based on recommendations of a Commission under Lord Diplock. The majority of these offences are also tried in the Crown Court on indictment but they are tried under procedures and rules of evidence which have been modified. The most important difference is that they are tried by a judge without a jury, the judge alone deciding all issues of fact as well as law, and passing sentence after conviction. The offences triable in this way are listed in Schedule 1 of the Northern Ireland (Emergency Provisions) Act 1991 and are referred to as 'scheduled' offences. The special non-jury Crown Courts are often referred to as 'Diplock' courts.

4. Some of the offences listed in Schedule 1 of the 1991 Act may be de-scheduled by the Attorney General certifying in a particular case that the offence is not to be treated as a scheduled offence. They should be de-scheduled if no element of terrorism was involved in their commission, but if the Attorney General refuses to de-schedule an offence there is no appeal against this decision. An example of an offence which should be de-scheduled is murder where it occurs in a domestic setting and is clearly unconnected with terrorist activity. Other offences are to be treated as scheduled only in particular circumstances, i.e. robbery, only where it is charged that an explosive, firearm, imitation firearm or weapon of offence was used in its commission. Some offences can never be de-scheduled; these include causing grievous bodily harm by explosives, withholding information about acts of terrorism and other offences clearly linked with terrorism by their very nature.

5. Whilst certain less serious offences, known as summary offences, must always be tried in a Magistrates' Court; and certain of the most serious offences, known as indictable offences must always be heard in the Crown Court; there is a third category of triable-either-way offences which, under one of three sets of circumstances, can be tried either in a Magistrates' Court or the Crown Court.

(a) Some offences normally tried summarily can be tried on indictment if the offence is one for which a person, if convicted, can be sent to prison for more than 6 months; and the defendant opts to be tried on indictment.

(b) Some offences which are normally tried on indictment can be tried summarily if the Magistrate considers that the case is not a serious one of its type and it is expedient to deal with it summarily; and the accused and the prosecution both agree to a summary trial. Petty theft and some types of assault fall into this category.

(c) In many cases the statute which creates a crime expressly states that it can be tried summarily or on indictment. It is then up to the prosecution bearing in mind the seriousness of the individual case, to decide which form of trial to use.

6. The mode of trial of scheduled offences depends on the general rules above, i.e. whether or not the offence is one which must be tried on indictment in the Crown Court or is a triable-either-way offence which will be tried summarily if the appropriate conditions are fulfilled. None of the scheduled offences fall into the category which must be tried summarily. Scheduled offences to be tried in the Crown Court are tried by a judge sitting alone without a jury. If they are dealt with in the Magistrates' court the procedure is the same as that for non-scheduled summary offences.

Magistrates' Courts

7. The vast majority of all criminal offences dealt with in Northern Ireland are tried summarily in a Magistrates' Court. Over half of these offences are offences against the Road Traffic (NI) Order 1981. It is estimated that where the defendant has a choice between summary trial and trial on indictment, approximately 3 out of 4 cases are dealt with summarily. This is mainly because this mode of trial is much quicker and the sentencing powers of a Magistrate are more restricted than those of a Crown Court judge - the most serious punishment which a Magistrate can impose is 12 months in prison, unless consecutive terms of imprisonment are imposed for more than one offence, when the limit is extended to 18 months.

8. The defendant has a right to appeal against his conviction or the sentence imposed upon him or both. The appeal takes place in the County Court before a County Court judge sitting without a jury. If the appeal is against conviction the accused will get a complete rehearing of his case. If the appeal is against sentence only the judge will review the sentence imposed by the Magistrate and affirm, reduce or increase it.

9. Appeals on a point of law from either the County Court or the Magistrates' Court go to the Court of Appeal. The Court of Appeal's ruling may be further challenged in the House of Lords, with leave from the Court of Appeal or the House of Lords.

Crown Court

10. Trial on indictment in the Crown Court follows after the accused has been returned for trial at committal proceedings in a Magistrates' Court. The Department of Public Prosecutions prepares a formal document called an indictment stating the charges which the accused will face. The matters are then tried before a judge sitting with a jury or if the offences are 'scheduled offences' sitting without a jury.

11. The Crown Court sits at nine different places throughout the province and trial of non-scheduled offences take place at the sitting of the Crown Court determined by the Magistrate who committed the accused, usually the Crown Court acting for the County Court division in which the offence is alleged to have been committed. All 'scheduled' offences are heard at the Crown Court sitting in Belfast.

12. Appeal from the Crown Court is to the Court of Appeal. The defendant can appeal on a point of law without obtaining the permission of any court. If he wishes to appeal against conviction on a question of fact he needs the permission of either the Crown Court judge or the Court of Appeal. If he wishes to appeal against sentence he needs the leave of the Court of Appeal.

13. All persons convicted of a scheduled offence tried on indictment can appeal against conviction to the Court of Appeal on any ground and without leave. This automatic right of appeal is a safeguard built into the system because in these cases there is no jury.

14. The prosecution have no right to appeal against the acquittal of a defendant who has been tried on indictment. The Attorney-General can refer a point of law to the Court of Appeal for its opinion, but even if the Court of Appeal considers that the trial judge made an error of law resulting in an acquittal, the acquittal still stands. The reference and subsequent ruling is useful in guiding the prosecution of future trials.

15. Further appeal by the defence or prosecution lies to the House of Lords. As with summary trials the leave of either the Court of Appeal or the House of Lords is required.

Juvenile Court

16. The Juvenile Court is a special Magistrates' Court constituted to deal with proceedings against children between the ages of 10 and 16. The Juvenile Court operates along broadly similar lines to the adult court, but with some differences:

(a) It consists of a bench of three members, of whom the chairman is a Resident Magistrate.

(b) Proceedings are held in private. Only persons connected with the case and court officials are present.

(c) The Juvenile Court can deal summarily with any indictable offence other than murder if it thinks that such a course is expedient and if the prosecution and the child's parents or the young person consents. It can make an order which might have been made by the Crown Court had the matter been tried on indictment.

(d) In addition to hearing criminal proceedings the court also hears proceedings relating to the care, protection and control of juveniles, though when a juvenile is charged jointly with an adult, charges will initially be heard in the ordinary Magistrates' Court.

Sentences available to the court

1. The types of sentence available to courts in Northern Ireland have evolved over the years with legislative change. Those available are outlined below. Sentencing to prison, Young Offenders Centre or a training school are collectively referred to as custodial disposals; probation orders, community service orders and attendance centre orders are collectively referred to as supervision orders.

| *Imprisonment* |

2. Imprisonment is the most severe penalty ordinarily available to the courts. The length of a term of imprisonment is determined either by statute or a judge or Magistrate in a common law case. It can vary from a few days to life, which is mandatory for a person convicted of murder. In Northern Ireland the maximum length of sentence that can be given by a Magistrate is 12 months for an indictable offence or 18 months if the person is convicted of more than one indictable offence.

3. Imprisonment is a sentence mostly confined to persons aged 21 and over (see Young Offenders Centre); but there is provision for detention of persons under 21 in a prison where the circumstances warrant it. Such detention is included in the statistics of imprisonment and can be for a stipulated sentence of over 4 years or at the Secretary of State's pleasure - analogous to a life sentence for persons under 18 when their crime was committed.

4. Prison sentences are rarely served in full. Remission may be granted at up to 50% of the sentence depending upon the circumstances, and 'lifers' may be released on licence at the decision of the Secretary of State. In murder cases the Secretary of State must consult the Lord Chief Justice and trial judge (if available).

| *Young Offenders Centre* |

5. Sentencing to the Young Offenders Centre is instead of imprisonment for persons under 21 who have been given custodial sentences of up to 4 years.

| *Training School Order* |

6. Training Schools are residential establishments approved under Section 137 of the Children and Young Persons Act (Northern Ireland) 1968 for the reception and training of children and young persons. They are also registered as remand homes. Duration of stay is determined by the Act but school managers have discretion to release persons on licence. The duration of stay may be up to 2 years in the case of someone under the age of 16. Persons over 16 may be detained until the age of 19. Some individuals attend the school on a daily basis only.

| *Suspended Sentence* |

7. This is a deterrent sentence, the term of which must not exceed 2 years. The period of suspension is between 1 and 3 years. If, during the suspension period, the offender commits an offence punishable by imprisonment, the court may order the suspended sentence (or a lesser term) to take effect. The court may also decide to impose a new suspension period or make no order with respect of the suspended sentence.

| *Community service Order* |

8. This Order requires the offender to do unpaid work in the community. It can be given to someone aged 16 or over convicted of an imprisonable offence if the offender consents and may be between 40 and 240 hours duration.

Attendance Centre Order	9. This Order deprives male juvenile offenders of some of their leisure time. This is usually a Saturday morning. It avoids removal from the home environment for extended periods.
Probation	10. The probation period may last for a period between 6 months to 3 years. It puts the offender under the supervision of a social worker and is not a punishment but a period during which probation personnel act as a source of guidance to avoid re-offending.
Fine	11. This is a financial punishment, the maximum level of which is generally set by statute. At common law the amount is unlimited. It is not a part of the principle of this sentence to fine a wealthy person according to their means. But it is thought desirable for the Magistrate to have some knowledge of the financial circumstances of the offender.
Deferred sentence	12. After conviction, a person may have the sentence deferred for a period of up to 6 months. Sentence is passed after changes (if any) in the circumstances of the case have been assessed. For example, the offender may have made some form of reparation.
Recognizance	13. This is called being 'bound over' and may be either 'bound over on own recognizance' or 'to keep the peace' or 'bound over on probation' etc. The offender and/or guarantors may enter into sureties which may be forfeited if the person re-offends.
Conditional Discharge	14. This Order imposes a condition upon the offender, i.e. that the offender commits no further offence for a specified period (1 to 3 years). If the condition is broken, the person may be dealt with for the earlier and the current offence.
Absolute Discharge	15. This may be imposed where punishment is considered inappropriate. The offender while found guilty is not further liable for the offence.

Other Publications

A series of statistical bulletins may be obtained from Statistics and Research Branch, Northern Ireland Office, Massey House, Stoney Road, Belfast. The series includes:

Crime Prevention - Results from the Continuous Household Survey

STATISTICS & RESEARCH BULLETIN 2/89

The International Victimisation Survey : A Northern Ireland Perspective

STATISTICS & RESEARCH BULLETIN 1/90

Imprisonment for Fine Default in Northern Ireland

STATISTICS & RESEARCH BULLETIN 2/90

Northern Ireland Prison Population Projections

STATISTICS & RESEARCH BULLETIN 3/90

The Financial Costs of Crime

STATISTICS & RESEARCH BULLETIN 5/90

The Risk of Victimisation in Northern Ireland

STATISTICS & RESEARCH BULLETIN 6/90

Reoffending by Persons Released from Prison in 1986

STATISTICS & RESEARCH BULLETIN 1/91

Operation of the Conditional Release Scheme

STATISTICS & RESEARCH BULLETIN 2/91

Crime in Northern Ireland 1982-1991

STATISTICS & RESEARCH BULLETIN 1/92

Court Proceedings in Northern Ireland 1982-1991

STATISTICS & RESEARCH BULLETIN 2/92

Sentencing Trends in Northern Ireland 1982-1991

STATISTICS & RESEARCH BULLETIN 3/92

The Northern Ireland Prison Population 1982-1991

STATISTICS & RESEARCH BULLETIN 4/92

Operation of the Northern Ireland (Emergency Provisions) Act 1991 for 1993

STATISTICS & RESEARCH BULLETIN 1/94

The Court of Appeal in Northern Ireland

STATISTICS & RESEARCH BULLETIN 1/95

The Use of the Fine in Northern Ireland

STATISTICS & RESEARCH BULLETIN 2/95

Also available are the following:

Digest of Information on the Northern Ireland Criminal Justice System -2

Statistics on the Police and Criminal Evidence (NI) Order 1989

STATISTICS & RESEARCH FACT SHEET 1/95

Northern Ireland Security Statistics 1994

STATISTICS & RESEARCH FACT SHEET 2/95

Experience of Drugs in Northern Ireland: Preliminary Research Findings from the 1994/95 Northern Ireland Crime Survey

RESEARCH FINDINGS 1/96